Cold War

A Captivating Guide to the Cold War and Space Race Between the United States and Soviet Union

Free Bonus from Captivating History (Available for a Limited time)

Hi History Lovers!

Now you have a chance to join our exclusive history list so you can get your first history ebook for free as well as discounts and a potential to get more history books for free! Simply visit the link below to join.

Captivatinghistory.com/ebook

Also, make sure to follow us on Facebook, Twitter and Youtube by searching for Captivating History.

Contents

Part 1: The Cold War

A Captivating Guide to the Tense Conflict between the United States of America and the Soviet Union Following World War II

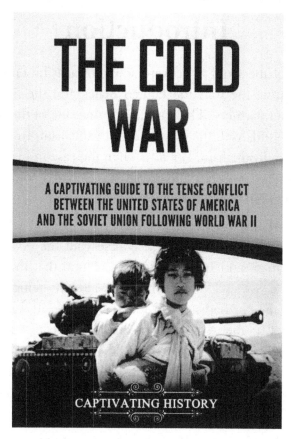

Introduction

The seeds of the Cold War were sown toward the end of World War II. During the war, the United States and the Soviet Union were reluctant partners. The communist doctrine of the Soviets was decidedly at odds with the US notion of capitalism, free enterprise, and rugged individualism. But as is often the case in history, despite their differences, America and Soviet Russia had a common enemy that brought them together—Nazi Germany.

And so, when Germany's ally, Imperial Japan, attacked the US, sending the nation on a collision course with the Axis Powers of Germany, Japan, and Italy, it was only natural that the Americans turned to the Soviet Union, which was already being fought to a standstill by the Nazi advance in Eastern Europe. It was due to the efforts to defeat the Axis that American misgivings about Soviet ideology were temporarily put to the side. And during the course of the conflict, American President Franklin Delano Roosevelt actually came to be on fairly good terms with the Soviet leader, Joseph Stalin.

During the war, strategy meetings—or summits as they were called—were held between FDR and Stalin, and the two seemed to develop quite a rapport with each other. It was a relationship that British Prime Minister Winston Churchill found troubling since

Churchill intuitively knew that a new conflict between the Soviets and free Europe would most likely begin immediately after the war's conclusion.

President Roosevelt abruptly perished in April of 1945, not living to see the end of World War II. When American ambassador William Averell Harriman famously informed Stalin of FDR's passing, Stalin was said to have seemed genuinely sad. Choking back his tears, the communist dictator, knowing that Harry Truman was next up for the presidency, steadfastly declared, "President Roosevelt has died but his cause must live on. We shall support President Truman with all our forces and all our will."

But soon after Truman took over the presidency of the United States, American and Soviet relations began to rapidly go south. Before the war was even over, disagreements arose over how the postwar world should be administered. The first real disagreement was over the main aggressor of the war—the defeated Axis power of Nazi Germany.

By May of 1945, America and her British ally jointly occupied Germany with Soviet Russia—a joint occupation that would turn into a partition based on ideological grounds. One side of Germany would be administered by the Russians, and it would be communist. The other would be administered by the Allies, and it would be a haven for democratic capitalism.

One of the first flashpoints in this occupation was over the massive influx of German refugees from the Soviet sector to the American zone. The Soviets and Germans had fought a very bitter war, with much bloodshed on both sides. Most of the German population, knowing that the Americans would be much more benevolent occupiers than the Russians, fled to the American side.

The Russians wanted to put a stop to this, and they asked the Americans to turn away asylum seekers. However, American military commanders often refused to cooperate. By the late 1940s, the Soviet Union had installed puppet governments in much of

Eastern Europe, including what would ultimately become East Germany. This epoch of communist consolidation is a moment that Winston Churchill captured quite well when he gave his famous "Iron Curtain" speech, also known as the "Sinews of Peace," on

March 5th, 1946.

During this speech, of which President Harry Truman himself was in attendance, Churchill famously declared that an iron curtain of tyranny had descended across Europe due to Soviet domination. Churchill's American allies, which were already at odds with the Soviets, took the speech fairly well. The Soviet Union, of course, did not. But Churchill's speech was not a call to arms as much as it was a progress report of the events that had been rapidly unfolding since the end of the war.

Churchill solemnly declared, "From Stettin in the Baltic to Trieste in the Adriatic, an iron curtain has descended across the continent. Behind that line lie all the capitals of the ancient states of Central and Eastern Europe. Warsaw, Berlin, Prague, Vienna, Budapest, Belgrade, Bucharest, and Sofia, all these famous cities and the populations around them lie in what I must call the Soviet sphere, and all are subject in one form or another, not only to Soviet influence but to a very high and, in some cases, increasing measure of control from Moscow."

Churchill's speech confirmed what many government officials in both the East and the West already felt. Less than a year after the end of the fires of World War II had been put out, the icy chill of another, more lasting conflict began to permeate the air. The Cold War had begun.

Chapter 1 – Berlin: The Lines Have Been Drawn

"Socialism is a philosophy of failure, the creed of ignorance, and the gospel of envy. Its inherent virtue is the equal sharing of misery."

-Winston Churchill

The city of Berlin dates back to the Middle Ages and has long been considered one of the most vibrant and cultured European cities, even during World War II. Sadly enough, Berlin, as was the rest of Germany, became hijacked by Hitler's Nazi Party. This previous center for literature, music, and art had its reputation terribly besmirched by the atrocities of Adolf Hitler. But even after the demise of Hitler on April 30th, 1945, Berlin's problems were far from over.

In the immediate aftermath of World War II, Berlin was jointly occupied by the United States and the Soviet Union, effectively splitting the city in two. Germany had already been split between East and West, but out of all the cities in Germany, Berlin's situation was the most precarious since the whole city was technically within Soviet-occupied territory.

Although West Berlin would remain free of Soviet dominion, it was an island of democracy surrounded by the communist-backed ideology of East Germany. The Soviets would maintain their stranglehold on Berlin for much of the rest of the Cold War, eventually building a wall right through Berlin and beyond. But perhaps one of the most harrowing yet inspiring moments in the Berlin standoff during the Cold War occurred in the summer of 1947, during the so-called Berlin Airlift, also known as *Berliner Luftbrücke* in German ("Berlin Air Bridge").

At this point, the sections of Germany previously controlled by the United States, Britain, and France had united into one entity known as West Germany. America was working hard to turn West Germany into a prosperous nation, even while the Soviets were forcing communist doctrine down the throats of East Germans. This flashpoint was intense, and things came to a head on June 24th, 1948, when the Soviets blocked the roads and rail lines that allowed access to the west side of Berlin.

This was done partly in response to the news that the Allies had established a new Deutsche Mark monetary currency in West Germany. The Soviets were against this. After World War II had come to a close, Soviet leader Joseph Stalin did not wish for an economically viable Germany to rise again. Now that the Western powers were helping to rebuild the economy of West Germany, not only was German financial stability being restored in West Germany, but it was also stoking Stalin's fear that a West German economic success would make East Germany wish to follow suit. He knew this would weaken his hold on the Soviet-controlled sector.

In a dramatic bid to make their displeasure known, the Soviets abruptly cut off access to Berlin. This was a severe provocation on the part of the Soviets since it could have led to an armed confrontation between American and Russian troops. And it seemed to all but head in that direction since many military leaders advocated sending armed convoys to the blocked roads to challenge the Soviet blockade.

But instead of risking this standoff, another idea was suddenly proposed. Thinking outside of the box, military planners began to consider what their options really were. And suddenly, it only made sense. If they could not reach Berlin by land, why not by air? This was how the idea of the Berlin Airlift—an effort to drop food, fuel, and medical supplies by air—came about. The airlift began in earnest on June 26th, 1948, when America and her Western allies began dropping their cargo over the city. This was a monumental effort, and at one point, nearly 13,000 tons of supplies were being delivered every day.

The operation officially came to a halt in the summer of 1949 after the Soviets ended their blockade of the overland routes to West Berlin. But even then, the Western Allies continued to drop supplies by air just in case the Soviets attempted to block off overland travel again. As such, the airlift did not actually come to a complete halt until the fall of 1949. It was a bitter standoff, and the stakes were much higher than most realized.

The United States and its allies were in a vulnerable position in Western Europe. Since the end of World War II, the military presence of the Western allies had been greatly reduced. Servicemen, of course, wanted to be home with their families, and since the war was ostensibly over, only a skeleton crew remained, which consisted of a few hundred thousand men. On the other hand, the Soviets never really reduced their numbers, and they had over one million troops at the ready. If the Soviets were to suddenly launch an attack, the Western defenders would have been pulverized.

However, the United States had the nuclear card up its sleeve. The US had developed the world's very first nuclear bomb at the tail end of World War II, ushering in the nuclear age by dropping two atomic bombs on Japan in 1945. The Soviets knew full well that the United States had a nuclear arsenal, but they doubted that they would use it. In 1948, the logistics of a successful nuclear attack on the USSR (Union of Soviet Socialist Republics) would have been difficult.

This was before the advent of ICBMs (intercontinental ballistic missiles), meaning an attack would have to been done in the same fashion as the bombing of Japan. This meant using heavy bomber planes to transport the weapons over Russian airspace and simply dropping the nuclear bombs from the plane. This cumbersome method would have been difficult even under optimal conditions. But since the Russians had a formidable air defense, the odds of the bombers getting shot down before deploying their nukes was considerably high.

Nevertheless, it was an option that President Harry S. Truman considered, as was evidenced when he sent B-29 bombers to Britain and had them remain on standby, just in case the decision was made for a bombing run. This was no doubt enough of a deterrent to make Stalin think twice about any further provocations, especially since the Soviets wouldn't create their first nuclear bomb until August 29th, 1949.

During the Berlin Airlift, the lines of the Cold War had become clearly drawn. It was during this operation that the North Atlantic Treaty Organization (NATO) was established. It was meant to be a concerted effort to shore up support between Western nations in the face of the Soviet threat. After the Berlin Airlift came to a close, West Germany was officially recognized as the "Federal Republic of Germany." The following year, the Soviets answered this by creating the so-called "German Democratic Republic" out of Soviet-controlled East Germany.

Since East Germany was becoming further isolated from the rest of the world, West Germany became increasingly integrated with its European neighbors. Closer ties between the Western nations were deemed necessary to stand strong against Soviet expansion and to serve as a measure to help prevent future hostilities in Western Europe. NATO was certainly a part of this, but so was the creation of the European Coal and Steel Community (ECSC), which, in many ways, laid the foundations of what would someday become the European Union (EU).

In 1951, the Treaty of Paris sealed the economic fates of West Germany, France, Italy, Luxembourg, Belgium, and Holland together for the first time in history. The ECSC, which was established through this document, created solidarity in the face of Soviet aggression. It had also been theorized that the more economically tied together the nations of Western Europe were, the less likely they would wage war on each other later on.

As of the writing of this book in the 2020s, this theory has proven to be correct. Although Western Europe had been the location of countless wars between Europeans in the past—including two world wars—from that day forward, there has not been any militarized aggression between the nations of Western Europe. They are more linked now than ever before. Eastern Europe has seen conflict since World War II, but Western Europe has not.

It is worth noting that even as Ukraine engages in a conflict with Russia in the 2020s, the Ukrainians are struggling to consolidate their solidarity with the European Union. They, too, would like to benefit from the economic and regional security that the EU provides. It was in the early days of the Cold War that the European Union began taking shape, with partitioned West Germany being its easternmost boundary.

Meanwhile, the Soviet Union was sponsoring its own conglomeration of Eastern European states by way of the so-called "Warsaw Pact." The Warsaw Pact, also known as the Warsaw Treaty Organization, was, as one might expect, forged in Warsaw, Poland. This agreement bound the Eastern Bloc countries of Poland, Romania, Hungary, East Germany, Czechoslovakia,

Bulgaria, and Albania together to form a collective defense of the region.

Western officials considered the Warsaw Pact to be somewhat meaningless since the Soviets already had agreements written up with all of the nations involved. But the Soviets wished to make a dramatic statement to the world, demonstrating that they had an armed camp of Eastern European communists to face off against the Western camp if they decided to attack. With NATO, the beginnings of the EU partnership, and the Warsaw Pact in place, the lines of the Cold War had been clearly drawn.

Chapter 2 – Stemming the Tide of Communism in East Asia

"If you want to know the taste of a pear, you must change the pear by eating it yourself. If you want to know the theory and methods of revolution, you must take part in revolution. All genuine knowledge originates in direct experience."

-Mao Zedong

Along with the fate of Western Europe, the status of East Asia soon became of concern during the Cold War. Even before World War II had officially come to a close, China had been simultaneously fighting off the Japanese while waging its own Civil War. The two main sides of this fraternal conflict were the Chinese Nationalists, led by Chiang Kai-shek, and the Communists, led by Mao Zedong. In the face of the greater threat of being conquered by Japan, there were moments of cooperation between these two factions, but these were only temporary lulls in their conflict against each other.

The Nationalists shouldered the biggest load since they were the main army to take on Japan. While the Communists stayed mostly holed up in remote regions resorting to guerilla warfare, China's

Nationalist army was right out in the open, slugging it out with Japan. Meanwhile, Mao Zedong and the other Communists would remain relatively safe, hiding out in the mountains.

The Nationalists would prevail against the Japanese in the end, but after having shouldered more than their fair share of the fighting, their numbers had been greatly reduced. Mao had been biding his time and shoring up the strength of his Red Army. After the defeat of Japan, what was left of the Nationalists and Mao's Red Army would ultimately enter into a state of all-out war with each other in the summer of 1946.

Despite Mao's numerical advantage, the Nationalists had much better equipment, as much of the equipment that the Communists used was outdated and obsolete. Although the Soviets were tacitly supporting the Communists, they did not yet want to rock the boat enough to supply arms to Mao.

At the very end of World War II, the Soviets had belatedly declared war on Japan, and they sent troops into what had been Japanese-controlled Manchuria in northeastern China. Upon Japan's surrender, Japanese military hardware came into the Soviets' possession, and they gifted this equipment to Mao's army. Mao's newly armed troops were then able to go on the offensive against the Nationalists. It was a bitter struggle, but the Chinese Communists eventually got the upper hand and drove the Nationalists right off the mainland.

What was left of the Nationalists sought refuge on the island of Taiwan, where they set up a provisional government based out of the Taiwanese city of Taipei. The administration based out of Taipei would call itself the Republic of China, or the ROC; this governmental body remains in place to this very day. Meanwhile, Mao Zedong declared victory on October 1ˢᵗ, 1949, marking the establishment of the People's Republic of China, the communist government that still rules mainland China today.

The repercussions of the Chinese Civil War are often forgotten, but it was similar to the division of East and West Germany, the partition of North and South Korea, and Vietnam. Just like those states, Taiwan was (and still is) a casualty of the Cold War's divisive ideologies. The Cold War was a polarizing epoch that split the world into two camps. You were either a communist or not.

Taiwan is essentially an extra-Chinese territory that broke away from the mainland in order to create an enclave free of Marxist dogma. Before the Japanese took over Taiwan, the land had been a part of China for centuries, but with the Japanese booted out, and the Nationalists with nowhere else to go, they made Taiwan a little place of their own. Although Chiang Kai-shek's grip on this outpost may have seemed like a tenuous one, as he was a man who fled the mainland in desperation, Taiwan has risen to be a regional player in its own right, and it is one of the most prosperous countries on the planet.

The success of the Chinese Communists on the mainland and their declaration of being an official communist state aligned with the Soviet Union was of deep concern to the Western powers. They immediately sought to contain the threat, lest communist ideology infect all of East Asia. Their resolve to contain the spread of communism faced its first major challenge in June of 1950 when communist North Korea sent its troops into Western-backed South Korea.

Korea had previously been a part of the Japanese Empire, but with Japan's defeat, the Korean Peninsula had been divided between the Western Allies and the Soviets, creating a communist-backed regime in the north and a capitalist/democratic government in the south. These territories were separated at the 38th parallel. Just like Germany, Korea had been divided and split in two between the ideologies of the two camps. North Korea, which was emboldened by China's success, felt it had the green light to attempt a forced unification under one communist Korean regime.

However, the United States was not going to just sit back and allow that to happen. As President Harry Truman stated at the time, "If we let Korea down, the Soviet[s]s will keep right on going and swallow up one [place] after another." In light of the aggression, the newly established United Nations gave authority to the United States and Britain to stop the incursion. US and British forces landed in South Korea shortly thereafter and quickly repelled the North Koreans.

Although the United States and its allies were able to push the North Koreans back, due to an endless supply line from both China and the Soviet Union, the North Koreans weren't going to give up any time soon. In addition to arms, the Chinese were also sneaking their own troops over the border, complicating matters even further. Considering all of these entanglements, Americans feared that a larger war between China and the Soviet Union could emerge, and they wished to end the conflict as soon as possible.

The fighting would continue as a stalemate for another few years until an armistice was agreed to in July of 1953. This agreement created a two-mile-wide buffer zone known as the DMZ (demilitarized zone) between North and South Korea. Interestingly enough, since no peace treaty was made, the Korean War never technically ended, making it the longest standing ceasefire the world has ever known.

After three years of fighting, five million people were dead, including some 40,000 Americans. Although the Allies were able to stop the spread of communism, they didn't gain anything. In fact, neither side really gained anything, as everything pretty much returned to the way it was before the bloodshed began. But the fact that the Western powers, namely America, were able to halt this forced communist advance was indeed a victory in for the US in the Cold War against the Soviets.

By this time, a new president had come to the White House in the form of President Dwight D. Eisenhower. Eisenhower, a

Republican, was a former army general and the Allied administrator of occupied Europe. A little over a month after Eisenhower was inaugurated as the new commander in chief, Soviet Premier Joseph Stalin died. Stalin, which was a Russian name he picked for himself, meaning "Man of Steel," had proven to the world that he was mortal after all. He passed fitfully away from a massive cerebral hemorrhage that caused a stroke.

In the early 1950s, another East Asian nation was making great strides. This time, it was not toward communism but toward a highly successful form of economic capitalism. This nation was Japan. The irony of the Cold War was the ultimate enemies of the United States during World War II—Germany and Japan—were rather rapidly rehabilitated after their defeat. Once they were revived, they sent aid to the US in its new struggle against the Soviets.

Upon their defeat, neither Germany nor Japan was allowed to have a military, but the political value of these former foes having successful democratic governments and strong economies proved to be of immense value. The better West Germany looked, the more it made East Germany and the Soviet Union look bad. The same went for East Asia. The better Japan did under capitalist directives, the more it made faltering North Korea look inferior.

The success of Japan in itself was a propaganda coup, and by the 1950s, the United States was pouring everything it could into this East Asian nation to make sure that it prospered. They called it the "Japanese Miracle," but US support had a lot to do with it. The United States knew that a happy and prosperous Japanese citizenry would be less likely to turn to communism or fascism. Furthermore, the US military presence in the region, in addition to a strong Japanese economy, stood guard against any Soviet advance into the Pacific.

Japan also directly benefited from the Korean War. Some might be surprised to hear this, but it's true. The US occupation of Japan proved to be pivotal in the war against North Korea since US troops could more easily shuttle back and forth between Japan and North Korea than if they deployed from the US or South Korea, which was under heavy bombing during the war. This meant that occupied Japan quickly became the number one supply depot of the war effort in Korea. The Japanese economy received a much-needed boost due to this commerce.

Of course, the United States can't take all the credit. Although it was US aid, business dealings, and stewardship that jumpstarted the Japanese economy, the Japanese played a key role in their own rapid development. Crucial to their recovery was the fast-tracking of companies that had previously served in Japan's military-industrial complex, which now moved over to the private sector. As a result, companies like Mitsubishi, which had previously been making fighter planes, were suddenly making cars.

Japan also cornered the market on electronics early on, funneling an enormous amount of time, money, and energy into the field. Due to this focus on consumerism, Japan would have the second-largest economy in the world by the 1960s, and it wouldn't begin to see a decline until late 1989.

Interestingly enough, it was during 1989/1990, when the Cold War began to thaw out, that Japan's rapid ascent started to stall. Japan would eventually rebound, but it would never see anything like the dramatic boom it had experienced during the post-WWII and Cold War years. At any rate, during the course of the Cold War, Japan served as the West's sentinel, standing as a capitalist bulwark that stemmed the tide of communism in East Asia.

Chapter 3 – Fighting the Soviets for Supremacy in Space

"We have learned how to navigate to the Moon. That is like the ancient Chinese mainlanders learning how to get Formosa; Formosa is the Moon. After we settle it, we jump off from there to Mars, just like they went next to the Philippines. And from there across our vast galaxy. If the Austronesians can sail in their boats and scatter into settlements across Oceania, we can take our spacecraft and scatter and settle across the Milky Way. It may take even longer than it took the Austronesians, but if they did it, so can we, because they are us."

-Neil Armstrong

After the passing of the Soviet Union's hardline dictator Joseph Stalin, Nikita Khrushchev became the new Soviet leader. Khrushchev's tenure would be marked by both saber-rattling and overtures of peace. He would also oversee a technological renaissance in the Soviet Union that would have the Russians kicking off the Space Race with the United States. The Space Race was a competition between the two great powers of the world, one democratic and one communist, to see who could dominate in the field of space exploration.

Khrushchev was the first to denounce the crimes of Joseph Stalin, who had wrongfully imprisoned, tortured, and killed countless Soviets. During a closed session of the Soviet Congress on February 25th, 1956, Khrushchev made his displeasure known. He proclaimed, "It is here that Stalin showed in a whole series of cases his intolerance, his brutality and his abuse of power. He often chose the path of repression and physical annihilation, not only against actual enemies, but also against individuals who had not committed any crimes against the party or the Soviet Government."

Khrushchev was determined to turn the page when it came to Soviet history, and most of his fellow Soviets seemed to be on board. There were a few demonstrations against Khrushchev in Stalin's native Georgia, but all in all, most seemed to want to move on just as much as Khrushchev did. Khrushchev still wanted to prove that the Soviet system was better than the American one, but he didn't want to fight World War Three to make his case. He just needed to find another outlet.

It wasn't long before he turned to science and the prospect of space exploration. Technically speaking, the Space Age had begun during World War II when the Germans launched a V-2 rocket outside the earth's atmosphere. The rocket was being used as a weapon at the time; in fact, it was the world's first long-range ballistic missile. Upon its reentry, the rocket slammed down onto military targets in Britain. But intended purpose aside, the V-2 was the first human-made object to leave the earth's atmosphere.

The Germans were the undisputed leaders in early rocketry, and it was from the Germans that both the United States and the Soviet Union gained much of their early hardware. Yes, before the Space Race even began, there was another race, one in which the two countries tried to get as much data off the Germans as they possibly could. The American effort in this regard began right after the war. It was codenamed Operation Paperclip. These efforts to glean the best in German technical know-how and personnel actually went on from 1945 all the way to 1959.

The Soviets had their own version of Operation Paperclip, which they called Operation Osoaviakhim. The name "Osoaviakhim" was actually an acronym for a Soviet military intelligence agency. The Soviet efforts to gain German expertise was much more aggressive than their American counterparts, and in some instances, Germans were forcibly seized.

One German engineer, Fritz Karl, described his experience in an interview he gave.

> Between midnight and 3 in the morning, when everybody was asleep. They knew exactly where I lived, first of all: a few days before I was captured, a fellow came. They had a key—they had everything to the apartment, to the door. There was one interpreter who told me, "Get up! You are being mobilized to work in Russia," and there were about half a dozen soldiers with machine guns, who surrounded me. When I wanted to get to the toilet, they checked it out first to make sure there was no escape hatch. It was a very tight operation.

As Karl's experience shows, if you were being "mobilized" to work for Russia, you really didn't have much choice in the matter. The United States' acquisition of top German scientists was a little different. If the Germans were not actively defecting to the US, they were typically persuaded to do so with promises of esteemed positions in America, where they could carry on their research. Not only that, the Americans promised to forgive and forget any undesirable incidents in their past, such as being implicated in war crimes.

This was famously the case with the man who would go on to run the Marshall Space Flight Center for NASA (National Aeronautics and Space Administration): Dr. Wernher von Braun. Von Braun was bagged by the Americans in the summer of 1945, along with several other "specialists." After being brought to America in the fall of 1945, von Braun and his associates had to have their troubled backgrounds "sorted out" by American officials. Most troubling was von Braun's work history, which included his overseeing the Peenemunde rocket base in Western Germany. This base utilized forced labor from concentration camps.

It still remains debatable how much blame should be placed upon von Braun. To some extent, he was under duress at the time since he would have most likely been killed or sent to a camp himself if he had refused to follow Nazi directives. Wernher von Braun was only working for the Nazi war machine out of necessity, as his true passion was to use his rockets for space exploration.

Still, no matter how one might try to spin it, having someone with such a tarnished past working for US special projects would not sit well with the general public, so it had to be covered up. For the most part, Wernher von Braun's skeletons were kept firmly locked in the closet. By 1950, he and his colleagues were quietly shuffled off to an army base in Huntsville, Alabama, where he would spend the next two decades continuing his research into rocketry.

For better or for worse, von Braun would be America's go-to-guy to take on the challenge of the Soviet Union's burgeoning rocket program. The Soviets missed out on nabbing von Braun thanks to the Americans, but they got the next best thing: his assistant, Helmut Gröttrup. Gröttrup had a strong background in physics, and he played a crucial role in the development of the V-2 rocket's "flight control system."

It is important to note that no one forced Gröttrup's hand. He actually chose to work for the Soviets of his own free will. Some say he was eager to get out from under von Braun and strike it out on his own; however, others contend it was simply a matter of logistics. He had a wife and children to worry about, and he did not want to move them out of Germany. The Soviets were allowing rocketry scientists who worked for them to stay in and around German territory. For some—especially those who could look past the darker side of communist Russia, ostensibly just as they had done with Nazi Germany—the closer commute was simply more appealing.

But the Soviets would betray these German scientists in the end and break their promise of a close commute. As the Cold War heated up, German scientists, such as Helmut Gröttrup, were shipped off to Russia. According to recently unearthed Soviet records, in the fall of 1946, some 7,000 Germans—approximately 500 rocket engineers among them—were forcibly transferred from Germany to Russia in order to work at Soviet-run facilities.

It was reported that Helmut was understandably angry with this betrayal. At one point, a frustrated Helmut asked the Soviet head of missile development, Dmitry Ustinov, when he and his compatriots could return home. To this, Dmitry offered the sarcastic remark, "As soon as you can fly around the world in a rocket!" This open mockery of his plight was certainly not what Helmut Gröttrup wanted to hear. Rather than being able to go home, Helmut was forced to work at the secretive Russian facility of Kapustin Yar, located near Kazakhstan. Irmgard captured the desolation of the environment of Kapustin Yar when she dryly noted in her diary that the "camels outnumbered the cars."

But nevertheless, despite the hardship of the remote location, the rocket scientists began to find their groove, and they even began to enjoy the work they were doing for the Russians. As the rocket tests began to get underway, Irmgard captured the excitement of the moment, writing in her journal that it felt "just like Peenemunde when we made our first experiments."

The Russians were not quite so enthralled by their German scientists. They were quick to drain them of all of their ideas, but once Russian scientists could replicate everything that the Germans taught, the Germans were callously discarded. It wasn't a German scientist that ended up running the Soviet space program but rather Ukrainian-born Sergei Korolev. Korolev had been involved with early Soviet research into rocketry in the 1930s, but he became ensnared in one of Stalin's infamous purges.

Sergei was sent to languish in work camps until he was finally released in 1944. After the war ended, Korolev was on the scene, overseeing the reverse engineering of German rockets and implementing designs of his own. The Soviets took his role so seriously that they wouldn't even divulge his name, keeping his identity a state secret. Sergei Korolev was known simply as "Chief Engineer."

Initially, the Russian aim when it came to rocketry—just like the American one—wasn't so much space flight as it was weapons of war. The Russians, in particular, were very interested in creating intercontinental ballistic missiles (ICBMs). With the genius Korolev at the helm, the Soviets were able to beat the Americans to the punch, conducting the world's first **ICBM** launch in 1957. But even while producing such impressive armaments for the Russian military, Korolev was actively seeking a way to apply his methods toward space exploration.

He found an opportunity when he heard reports that America was considering putting a satellite in space. Korolev sought out Soviet Premier Khrushchev and told him of these happenings and his concern that the Soviets were falling behind. Not to be outdone, Khrushchev gave Korolev permission to embark upon a satellite project. After being given the green light, Korolev went full throttle into an engineering project that would result in the launching of Sputnik 1, the world's first orbiting satellite, in 1957

Today, the idea that satellites orbit the earth is a pretty mundane reality of everyday life. But back then, the idea that the Russians had an object that could fly right over America—albeit from space—was frightening. Americans were soon clamoring for a response. It was due to that little satellite named Sputnik that the Space Race began in earnest. Incensed by the orbiting object, von Braun's handlers in the United States had him rush into development of the American version, which was called Explorer 1.

This satellite was rapidly launched in January of 1958 in order to show the Soviet Union that America could meet them in orbit. In January of 1959, the Soviets decided to up the ante by sending a satellite that not just orbited Earth but also broke free of Earth's gravity altogether to orbit the sun. In the summer of 1959, Wernher von Braun and his American handlers then took the initiative to launch Explorer 6, which would have the honor of taking the very first photograph of Earth from space.

As you can see, the competition of space firsts was in full swing by this point. One achievement on one side was quickly followed by another from the other side. And before the year was out, the Russians had sent a craft to the Moon (it actually crashed right into it), followed by another, which flew by taking snapshots of the Moon's far side. With these rapid achievements, the US felt as if it was lagging behind. For the top brass in the United States military, the achievement gap wasn't just demoralizing for space exploration, but it also presented a real threat to national security.

We may laugh about it now, but there was a serious fear back then that the Russians would establish a base on the Moon and use it to launch attacks on Earth, namely on the US. Taking these fears into consideration, even before John F. Kennedy pledged to send Americans to the Moon before the decade was out, von Braun and his fellow German scientists were quietly taken to the headquarters of the recently created National Aeronautics and Space Administration (NASA) in 1960. At the time, it was centered around the Marshall Space Flight Center in Huntsville, Alabama.

Here, they were given a "mandate" to design a rocket that would be able to take American astronauts to the Moon. Shortly after his arrival, von Braun was made the "chief designer" of what would become the Saturn V rocket. Wernher von Braun employed another former Nazi, Arthur Rudolph, who had worked with him back in Germany as an operations director for the V-2 rocket. As the Saturn V concept continued to be refined and developed, it was determined that it would need a separate launch complex.

For this purpose, land was acquired in Florida. Cape Canaveral, located on the eastern side of Florida, was chosen as the launch site for future prototypes. In order to have a hanger for the massive Saturn V, the Vertical Assembly Building was built on tiny Merritt Island, situated just off the mainland of Florida. This massive warehouse was fashioned by another German rocket expert and colleague of von Braun, Bernhard Tessmann.

But even while all of these plans were being made, the Soviets still held the lead, and they maintained it in a spectacular way in April of 1961 when they launched the first man—Yuri Gagarin—into orbit. This was particularly galling to the newly elected American president, John F. Kennedy, since he had run for office on a platform declaring that he would finally "close the gap" in the Space Race. This moment made Kennedy more determined than ever to put a man on the Moon and to do so *before* the Soviet Union.

But, in the meantime, they were still playing catch-up. After Gagarin successfully orbited the planet, NASA sent American astronaut Alan Shepard up into space on May 5th, 1961. It must be noted that Shepard was the first American in space, but he wasn't the first American to orbit Earth. That honor belongs to John Glenn, who circled Earth in orbit in February of 1962. At this point, the American space program was making some rather rapid strides, but they still had their work cut out for them if they wanted to beat the Soviets.

In order to achieve Kennedy's vision of a man on the Moon before the decade was out, NASA received a massive influx of cash from the federal government between 1961 and 1964. NASA made some major inroads during this period, but tragedy would strike in 1967 when three crew members—Gus Grissom, Ed White, and Roger Chaffee—died in a fiery explosion while testing out a piece of equipment. NASA was both saddened and embarrassed by the debacle, and the Soviets hailed it as yet another sign that the Americans were woefully behind in the Space Race.

But in reality, even though America was open and forthcoming with any accidents that befell them, the Soviets simply kept a tight lid on their mishaps so that the rest of the world would never find out about it.

For instance, Russian cosmonaut Vladimir Komarov came crashing down to Earth on April 24th, 1967. The craft he went up on—Soyuz 1—is said to have been beset with a wide variety of technical problems. The craft's electric power stalled when a solar panel failed, and antennas failed to properly deploy, interfering with navigation. Despite these hardships, Komarov was a skilled enough pilot to successfully wade through these problems and steer the craft back into Earth's atmosphere for reentry. The final flaw of this ill-prepared craft was when the ship's landing parachutes failed to deploy properly, causing the doomed astronaut to slam right into the surface of the earth. In the end, all that remained of the doomed cosmonaut were charred bones and ashes.

According to the official narrative, this sudden impact is the end of the story. But there is a conspiracy theory, which has been in circulation for a number of years now, that there is more to this account. This theory alleges that Vladimir Komarov knew that he was doomed from the beginning, that he knew full well that the craft's production had been haphazardly rushed.

Chief Designer Korolev had died the year before, and many Soviet projects had since become streamlined and hurried along by Korolev's less cautious successors. If Komarov had suspected the craft was flawed, he obviously felt that he could not say no. This scenario was described by Jamie Doran and Piers Bizony in 2011 in their book *Starman*. The book then goes on to make the far more sensational claim that American intelligence operatives stationed in Turkey were able to pick up transmissions of Komarov's last words to Russian ground control. Komarov was supposedly "crying with rage," cursing the botched job that the Soviet engineers had done on his craft. So, who was the supposed source of all these riveting details? According to the book, it was a former KGB operative named Venyamin Russayev, whose identity has not actually been confirmed.

Conspiracy theories involving the Soviet space program (and even the American one) are nothing new. For several decades now, the "Lost Cosmonauts" theory has been propagated. This theory claims that several cosmonauts were sent out before Yuri Gagarin. These men died and are either still orbiting the earth or were sent hurtling out into deep space. As fascinating as all this might be for science fiction, this book will stick to scientific facts. As it stands, all we really know of the ill-fated flight of Vladimir Komarov is that his parachutes failed, the craft crashed, and he perished in the inferno.

At any rate, the Soviets continued their quest for dominance, and they ramped up their race to the Moon in the aftermath of Komarov's death. In 1968, they launched Zond 5, a robotic craft that carried not humans but a couple of tortoises, sending them circling around the Moon. Although this is not as exciting as human flight, it was another first that could be credited to the Soviets. This was the first time that any lifeforms from Earth had been sent into lunar orbit and returned safely home.

Besides the propaganda victory, the mission revealed little more than what the Soviets already knew. The most important details gleaned was in regard to the effects of radiation—if any—on terrestrial life. Other than being a little hungry, the turtles proved to be unaffected by space travel. But although they survived the return trip back to Earth, these heroic tortoises wouldn't live much longer. They were promptly dissected by Soviet scientists, as they wished to study the effects of outer space on their organs.

In the meantime, NASA, not wanting to be left behind again, decided to one-up the Soviets. Before the end of the year, the US made history by sending not turtles but human beings to circle the Moon on Apollo 8. Kennedy's promise to send Americans to the surface of the Moon before the end of the decade seemed just within grasp.

The Soviets, seeming to already admit defeat when it came to the race to the Moon, suddenly switched gears. Instead of focusing on the Moon, they achieved another historic first in another arena with the first docking of two manned craft and the first exchange of crew members between two docked crafts. These are both very important milestones, as they would be crucial for the later operation of space stations, which require crafts to be able to securely dock to the station.

Nevertheless, despite these triumphs of Soviet science, NASA would steal all the glory by ultimately placing the first human beings onto the surface of the Moon in 1969. The whole world watched in wonder as human beings stepped out onto an alien world for the very first time. This would be the final, stunning conclusion of the Space Race. Not a shot was fired, yet America had seemingly won the war in space.

Chapter 4 – How the Cold War Calculus Affected the Middle East

"Israel is the one country in which everyone is pro-American, opposition and coalition alike. And I represent the entire people of Israel who say, 'Thank you, America.' And we're friends of America, and we're the only reliable allies of America in the Middle East."

-Benjamin Netanyahu

Although you might not know it if you flipped on the mainstream news, which, at least as of this writing, seems to be underreporting one of the biggest news stories of 2020: the peace deals made between Israel, the UAE (United Arab Emirates), and Bahrain. These two Arab Gulf State countries had been sworn enemies of Israel since the nation's creation in 1948. Like many countries in the Middle East at the time, both the UAE and Bahrain held a hostile stance toward Israel.

Israel's creation, although not directly linked to the conflicting ideologies of the Cold War, quickly became a centerpiece in the struggle between the Cold War powers. The Soviets wished to use

Arab resentment of the creation of Israel to its advantage when dealing with the West. And even though the Middle East players may not have been direct communist sympathizers, they, too, were willing to play one superpower off the other.

In order to understand how the Cold War calculus affected the Middle East, one first needs to understand how the modern state of Israel came into existence. Getting into the full history of the region would be beyond the scope of this book, so this will be as brief as possible.

The Jewish claim to Israel goes back to the days of the Bible, around 1,000 years before Christ. Then fast forward to the days of Jesus—around 30 CE—and Israel was part of the Roman Empire. Jews still lived in the land, but the ultimate control rested in the hands of Roman governors. It was an uneasy relationship, and things came to a head in the Bar Kokhba Revolt of 132 CE. This was a major uprising against Roman authority, in which Jewish leader Bar Kokhba raised up an army of some 200,000 fighters to take on Rome's military might.

The results for Bar Kokhba, his followers, and all of the residents of Israel were not good. All of Bar Kokhba's men were either put to death or sent off to Rome in chains. In all, about half a million Jews were killed, and the survivors were expelled from Jerusalem. Roman Emperor Hadrian was so incensed by the rebellion that he sought to root out all aspects of Judaism from the land. Hadrian denied the practice of the Torah and outlawed Jewish customs. Seeking to literally wipe Israel off the map, Hadrian then renamed the land "Syria Palaestina," which would eventually become known as simply "Palestine."

Now flash forward to 325 CE. This was the year Roman Emperor Constantine held the Council of Nicaea and began making laws that were favorable to Christianity. Before Constantine, Christians were routinely persecuted, but after Constantine, they would flourish. Christians then moved into Israel/Palestine, built churches, and Christianized the region, honoring it as the land that Christ had once walked.

Christian dominance in Israel/Palestine lasted until the 7th century when the Persians took over the territory. The Persian occupation proved to be brief, as they were driven out in 625. But Roman Christians wouldn't have long to celebrate before a new powerful force called Islam rose up in Arabia and assailed the region in the late 630s.

Israel/Palestine ultimately fell to the forces of Islam and would remain in Muslim hands until the time of the First Crusade in the late 1090s. Crusaders would reside in the Holy Land until they were finally driven out by Islamic forces roughly 200 years later in the 1290s. The land of Israel/Palestine would then be ruled by several different Muslim leaders until finally being consolidated under the Islamic powerhouse of the Ottoman Empire in 1516. The Ottomans would then rule the land until around 1918, which was when the Ottoman Empire was defeated in World War I.

The Ottomans had picked the wrong side of the war by aligning themselves with the Central Powers of Germany, Austria-Hungary, and Bulgaria. Upon their defeat, the British took over control of Palestine. Britain then created a mandate in which they promised to create "an eventual homeland for Jews in Palestine." It is said that by the time this mandate was ratified in 1922, only about 58,000 Jews actually lived in the region. But by the end of the decade, the number began to increase rapidly.

As Jewish immigration intensified, so, too, did local Arab resentment. Despite traditional Jewish history dating back thousands of years, the current local residents did not recognize any Jewish claim to the land. And soon, there were outright riots and revolts staged by Arab leaders against the Jews. Nevertheless, the immigration continued, and so did calls for Britain to recognize a Jewish state. Britain, worried about inflaming tensions in the region even further, hesitated to do so.

It wasn't until the end of the Second World War that an American-backed plan came into being to finally create a Jewish state. It was in light of the horrors of the Holocaust that much of the world became determined to facilitate a homeland for the Jews. When the matter was brought to the United Nations, even the Soviet Union came out in favor of a plan to partition Palestine into a Jewish state. Most seemed to feel that the Jews deserved a safe haven of their own after having so much pain and suffering inflicted upon them during the war.

Soviet ambassador Andrei Gromyko probably summed up this sentiment best in an address to the United Nations.

As we know, the aspirations of a considerable part of the Jewish people are linked with the problem of Palestine and of its future administration. This fact scarcely requires proof. During the last war, the Jewish people underwent exceptional sorrow and suffering. The United Nations cannot and must not regard this situation with indifference, since this would be incompatible with the high principles proclaimed in its Charter. The fact that no Western European state has been able to ensure the defense of the elementary rights of the Jewish people and to safeguard it against the violence of the fascist executioners explains the aspirations of the Jewish to establish their own state. It would be unjust not to take this into consideration and to deny the right of the Jewish people to realize this aspiration.

However, this sympathy was not shared by Israel's Arab neighbors, and when Israel was declared a nation on May 14th, 1948, an all-out war was launched against them. Yes, Israel had only been a nation for less than a day before having to fend off an onslaught from several Arab countries all at once. Israel was ready, and it surprised the world by not only surviving the attack but actually gaining ground. This round of hostilities ended in a truce in March of 1949, but Israel's enemies still refused to recognize Israel as a legitimate state.

It was in their rage and anguish over Israel's statehood that many Arab powers began to turn to the Soviet Union for support. Initially, the Soviets hoped that they could influence policies in Israel, but when this proved unlikely, they began to turn to the Arabs instead. First among the Arab countries that the Soviets courted was Egypt. The rise of Egyptian leader Gamal Abdel Nasser, who was a staunch anti-imperialist, was met with approval by the Soviets.

By 1955, the Russians were actively supplying arms to Egypt. Most importantly, after Nasser decided to nationalize the Suez Canal, he was backed up to the hilt by the Soviets. The Suez Canal was built in the 19th century by the British when Egypt was still under British colonial rule. After Egypt gained independence from the British, Egyptian nationalists began to call for the nationalization of the Suez Canal, which was still being administered by both the British and the French. Things came to a head in 1956 when Gamal Abdel Nasser did just that.

This move prompted a joint invasion by Britain and France in an attempt to force access to the canal—an invasion that was preceded by an Israeli incursion into the Sinai. These actions would have ramifications on a global scale, as the Soviets mobilized to back their Egyptian client state. The Soviet Union threatened military action and even a nuclear exchange if the belligerents didn't leave Egypt in peace. This prompted the United States to weigh in and order all of the belligerents to leave Egypt at once.

US President Eisenhower was afraid that the situation in Egypt would lead to nothing short of World War Three, and he wasn't willing to allow such a thing to happen on his watch, especially over this distant piece of real estate. It was a humiliating blow to British prestige in particular (it was now clear that British domination had long since passed), but both Britain and France acquiesced and withdrew their troops.

Israel, on the other hand, would not leave the Sinai until 1957. They would later return, with the final withdrawal from the region only coming after the Egypt-Israel Peace Treaty of 1979. The fact that the Soviets had stood so strongly for Egypt, which apparently alarmed the United States enough to get them to pressure the aggressors to back down, was a major propaganda victory for Soviet Russia.

The Soviets, riding high on this political victory, would use it to portray themselves as the champions of the underdog and the protectors of less-developed nations against imperialism. For the Soviets, this was the moment when the West blinked. For at the mere threat of Soviet retaliation, the United States was convinced to rein in its allies.

But to say that Soviet pressure caused the US to blink is a rather unfair portrayal because it must be recognized that America was against the invasion of Egypt in the first place. President Eisenhower's British, French, and Israeli allies had essentially gone rogue and conducted an operation without his consent. So, it wasn't so much that the Eisenhower administration blinked as it was that they made good on their intentions to get their allies back in order.

Unlike the Cuban Missile Crisis of the 1960s, in which the Soviets famously reversed course under American pressure, the Suez Crisis was not of American design—instead, America was simply pulled into the fray. But, of course, reality and how reality is perceived are often two different things. And when it came to the Cold War calculus of the Middle East, perception was everything.

Chapter 5 – Cuba, Vietnam, and Increasing Social Unrest

"Reactionaries often describe both Marx and Lenin as theorists, without taking into consideration that their utopias inspired Russia and China—the two countries called upon to lead a new world which will allow for human survival if imperialism does not first unleash a criminal, exterminating war."

-Fidel Castro

As the Eisenhower administration was coming to a close in the late 1950s, an unexpected focal point of the Cold War was beginning to emerge just some ninety miles from the Florida coast in a little-known place called Cuba. In previous years, Cuba had been run by American-friendly dictatorships, the latest of which was helmed by a guy named Fulgencio Batista. Batista's rule abruptly came to an end when a revolutionary by the name of Fidel Castro managed to orchestrate a coup.

The American CIA (Central Intelligence Agency) knew that Batista's days were numbered, but they didn't want a radical bunch of revolutionaries taking over. So instead, they attempted to engineer a transition to a new leader, hoping that a new face would calm down the clamor of the Cuban public. The Americans backed Cuban General Eulogio Cantillo, who brokered a ceasefire and announced that Batista would step down from power. Cantillo told the Cuban people that Batista would be arrested, but in reality, he was given safe passage out of Cuba, leaving on December 31st, 1958.

The next day, General Cantillo, acting as a kingmaker, tapped a former Supreme Court judge by the name of Carlos Piedra to step in to head a transitional government until a proper election could take place. But if the Pentagon hoped that the Cuban revolutionaries would be happy with this arrangement, they were mistaken. Castro and his revolutionaries were none too pleased by these developments, and they proceeded to head right for Havana—the capital of Cuba—to sort it out for themselves.

Upon getting to the capital, Castro and his associates rounded up General Cantillo, thew him in jail (he was released a few years later and fled to Florida), and then took over the power themselves. At first, Fidel Castro tried to distance himself from communism. When he visited the United States in 1959, he denied believing in any part of communist ideology. Fidel Castro intended to meet with American President Eisenhower during his visit, but he ended up having to settle for Vice President Richard Nixon instead. Castro and Nixon seemed to rub each other the wrong way from the start, and Nixon did not believe for one second that Castro was not being influenced by communism.

After their meeting, Nixon would say Castro "was either incredibly naïve about communism or under communist discipline—my guess is the former." After Castro returned to Cuba, the relations between the United States and the new Cuban government continued to be strained. By the time a young senator from Massachusetts by the name of John F. Kennedy was elected to succeed Eisenhower, communication between the US and Cuba had ceased.

Kennedy had run his campaign with a pledge that he would do something to improve the situation in Cuba. Now, he had to put his money where his mouth was. In his effort to avoid a Cold War loss of Cuba falling to communism, Kennedy cobbled together a group of Cuban exiles in an attempt to facilitate the ousting of the Castro regime. These efforts would culminate in the Bay of Pigs fiasco in 1961. The name of the operation stemmed from where these operatives landed, which was on the part of Cuba known as the "Bay of Pigs."

In order to prevent a Cold War confrontation, Kennedy made sure to keep the operation a strictly Cuban affair, one with only Cuban fighters involved. In the end, the operation was a dismal failure, and all of the Cuban exiles were either killed or captured. The US already suspected Castro of being a communist ideologue, and after the Bay of Pigs, he made it loud and clear. Castro went on the record and famously declared that he was a Marxist the day after the botched Bay of Pigs invasion.

Castro was now openly engaging with the Soviets and had become the latest major pawn in the Cold War. With Kennedy's administration secretly plotting to overthrow the regime, Castro asked the Soviets for assistance. He probably expected to be gifted with conventional arms, but to his own surprise, the Soviets suggested that nuclear missiles be placed on the island as a deterrent.

Soviet Premier Nikita Khrushchev was still flying high on his ability to apply pressure on the US during the Suez Crisis from several years before, and he thought it was about time that he tried his luck again. Khrushchev believed that Kennedy was no match for Eisenhower, and if Eisenhower was easy to push around, Khrushchev must have believed messing with Kennedy would be child's play. But he was mistaken, and soon Kennedy would show the Soviets just how tough his resolve really was.

After U-2 spy plane images confirmed that Cuba had nuclear missiles, Kennedy took his concerns right to the public. On live TV, he revealed to the world what the Soviets had done. He then made his own intentions crystal clear. Kennedy declared that if a nuclear missile was shot from Cuba, the US would not only hold the Soviets accountable but would also unleash America's nuclear arms upon the Soviet Union itself. It was Khrushchev this time around that would "blink."

Not wishing to risk nuclear war over Cuba, Khrushchev immediately reached out to Kennedy to cut a deal. Behind the scenes, Kennedy agreed to remove some nukes that had been stored in Turkey in exchange for the Soviets removing the nuclear weapons from Cuba. In order to placate Cuba, Khrushchev even managed to get a pledge from Kennedy that he would cease any and all attempts to overthrow the Castro regime. There would be no more nukes on Cuban soil, but there would also be no more Bay of Pigs-styled invasions for Castro to worry about either.

This should have made all parties happy, but Castro ended up feeling insulted and slighted. He was particularly infuriated that the US and the USSR conducted this agreement without even consulting him in the first place. Fidel also criticized Khrushchev for looking "weak" in the exchange with the Americans. Castro thought that the Americans had won this round of the Cold War far too easily.

But another great test of the Cold War was heating up around this time in Vietnam, and this one would not be so easily passed. Vietnam had gone through a tremendous social upheaval since the time of the Second World War. Prior to World War II, Vietnam was a French colony. After France fell to Nazi Germany in World War II, France found much of its former colonial empire in quite a precarious state.

After surrendering to the Nazis, the French Vichy government came to power. It sided with Hitler, and according to the terms of this new partnership, Vichy France would be allowed to keep and maintain its colonies. Germany's partner in the Axis, Japan, had other plans. As the Japanese spread through East Asia, conquering one territory after the other, the Japanese began to put more and more pressure on Vichy France to give them territorial concessions.

When Japan eventually decided to seize control of French Vietnam for its own purposes, Hitler turned a blind eye and allowed the Japanese to proceed without any argument, proving just how bad a deal with Hitler could be. Japan allowed the French to carry out some of their former administrative duties in running the place, but with Japanese troops on every corner, there was no question who was in charge. A home-grown resistance movement of Vietnamese fighters, which consisted of local communists called the Viet Minh, rose up and began to wage guerrilla warfare against the Japanese.

The United States actually backed the Viet Minh at this point since they were an ally in the fight against Japan. However, once Japan had been defeated after World War II came to a close, all hell broke loose when the French attempted to reassert their authority over Vietnam. The communist Viet Minh, who had been struggling to rid their land of Japanese troops, weren't about to resubmit to French dominion—they wanted independence.

The United States, which was generally against colonies by this point (the US had pressured Britain to let go of several of theirs after the war) and all for independent democratic nations, was initially supportive of their war-time ally, the Viet Minh. But as the Cold War began to take hold, US officials realized that the Viet Minh wanted to turn Vietnam into a hardline communist state. The Americans were aghast and began to support the French. France proved to be no match for the communists, however, and ended up pulling out of Vietnam altogether.

In 1954, just as had occurred in Germany and the Korean Peninsula, Vietnam was divided into two countries: the communist

North and the democratic capitalist South. In the Geneva Conference that followed the French withdrawal, the Soviets actually pressured the Vietnamese communists to accept the proposed partition, arguing that it would give them time to stabilize and shore up their strength.

Nevertheless, it wasn't long before the North turned on the South and began battling for complete dominance of Vietnam. This was a clear trespass against the United States policy of containment, and just as had been the case with Korea, the US felt compelled to step in. The US would not immediately put troops on the ground; initially, the United States simply supplied weapons and other supplies to the South Vietnamese, hoping that this extra bit of help would be enough for them to defeat North Vietnam on their own.

But when the South seemed to be on the verge of collapse by the early 1960s, the United States decided it was time to take decisive action. In February 1965, US President Lyndon B. Johnson authorized a bombing campaign that would become known as Operation Rolling Thunder. That same year, communist China sent engineers to bolster defenses in North Vietnam, making structural repairs to airstrips, railways, and other important infrastructure—the very targets of Operation Rolling Thunder.

Less than a month after Operation Rolling Thunder commenced, the first US combat troops stepped foot in South Vietnam. They were ordered to guard US air bases in the region. By the summer of 1965, the number of US troops in Vietnam would grow to over 100,000. Meanwhile, China would end up placing hundreds of thousands of Chinese troops, who hid among the Vietnamese fighters, in Vietnam over the next few years.

Although this was a full escalation of the conflict, the United States still had to play its cards very carefully, lest it pull itself into a direct fight with China or the Soviet Union. The Soviets, for their part, kept their aid to North Vietnam fairly discreet, but as the conflict progressed, so did their support. Their support actually increased after Leonid Brezhnev, who was determined to better flex the Soviet Union's military muscle, succeeded the disgraced Nikita Khrushchev, who lost much of his credibility with his fellow Soviets after the Cuban Missile Crisis.

In 1965, the Soviets agreed to a defense treaty with the North Vietnamese, which would guarantee financial aid, military hardware, and technical advisors to assist the Vietnamese communists in their struggle. The Soviets were now coming right out into the open with their support. And if there was any confusion, the Soviet Union issued a public statement declaring the following:

> The Democratic Republic of Vietnam (DRV), the outpost of the socialist camp in south-east Asia, is playing an important role in the struggle against American imperialism and is making its contribution to the defense of peace in Asia and throughout the world. The governments of the USSR and DRV have examined the situation. Both governments resolutely condemn the aggressive actions of the USA—and especially the barbaric attacks by American aircraft on DRV territory. The USSR will not remain indifferent to ensuring the security of a fraternal socialist country and will give the DRV necessary aid and support.

This statement made it clear to the world that the Soviets considered it their duty to protect the fledgling communist country. And by the end of the decade, it's said that about three-quarters of all aid given to the North Vietnamese was from the Soviets. However, the Soviet Union was about to run into an issue. It was not its support of Vietnam that was the problem, but rather China's involvement with Vietnam.

Since both the Soviets and the Chinese were communists, one would think they would be natural allies. Yet ever since the late 1950s, the two communist juggernauts had begun to drift into two different directions. From that point forward, they were more likely to compete with one another than actually collaborate together. By

1968, these tensions had reached a dangerous boiling point that saw Soviet soldiers mobilizing on the Chinese border.

These tensions would erupt in 1969 in a border skirmish that would leave some 200 people dead. Although the Soviet Union and China never officially went to war, this violent onslaught was about as close as you could get without actually calling it that. As volatile as Soviet/Chinese relations had become, toward the end of the Vietnam War, it got to the point where Vietnam basically had to decide on whether it would get the lion's share of its support from the Soviets or from the Chinese.

Since the Soviets had better military equipment at the time, it wasn't too difficult of a decision to make. When the preference of the Vietnamese became known, Mao Zedong began to scale back support and had Chinese troops begin to make their exit. By this point, Vietnam appeared to have an "endless river" of supplies and resources flowing forth from the Soviet Union.

As such, the idea that America could actually win in this bloodbath began to come into doubt. But even before military handlers would admit the Vietnam War was not working, the American people already knew. There was increasing unrest in the streets because of it. There had been sporadic protests against the war since the early 1960s, but it wasn't until after the Tet Offensive, which took place in 1968, that protests at home really began to gain traction.

The Tet Offensive was a major assault conducted by the North Vietnamese that took the fight to over one hundred different sites in South Vietnam. This all-out attack was meant to shatter American morale and encourage the South Vietnamese to defect. For the most part, the North Vietnamese were successful in these aims. American troops were eventually able to repel the North Vietnamese, but once these events reached the American public via the news media, many Americans began to doubt the chances of the United States ever beating the North Vietnamese.

It seemed that no matter how many Vietnamese died in these brazen attacks, they would just send more, perpetuating an endless bloody stalemate. In fact, esteemed newsman Walter Cronkite voiced that same sentiment when he remarked over media coverage that it appeared "more certain than ever that the bloody experience of Vietnam is to end in a stalemate." This prompted President Lyndon B. Johnson to famously lament, "If I've lost Cronkite, I've lost Middle America."

And Johnson appeared to have been right in his estimation of events because it was this realization that Vietnam was a war with no end in sight that would lead even those who weren't against the war on ideological grounds to consider the whole thing a lost cause. With such a rapid loss of confidence in the war, protests became a regular occurrence. In light of these happenings, the disillusioned LBJ wouldn't even seek a second term in 1968, instead leaving the task of a new presidential candidate to other Democrats.

In the lead-up to the 1968 election, the United States would become a seething hotbed of social unrest. There were not only protests over the Vietnam War but also widespread protests and riots over civil rights issues. The leader of the modern civil rights movement, Reverend Martin Luther King Jr., had been assassinated on April 4th, 1968. His death was met with anger and anguish, and many American cities went up in flames.

In the meantime, the Democratic Party was trying to figure out who would run for president in LBJ's place. By the spring of 1968, the Democratic front-runners were Senator Eugene McCarthy, Senator George McGovern, Senator Robert F. Kennedy, and LBJ's vice president, Hubert Humphrey. In a field like this, a former vice president usually has the most clout, as vice presidents, if they decide to run, tend to succeed the president they served under.

But Hubert Humphrey was up against Robert F. Kennedy in the primaries, and Kennedy was extremely popular. The American public was deeply saddened when Robert's brother, President John

F. Kennedy, had been assassinated in 1963. They could see the slain former president's passion and ideals in Robert Kennedy, and many hoped that Robert could restore some of what John F. Kennedy's magical Camelot days in Washington had lost.

After Robert Kennedy won the California primary in 1968, he seemed poised to surpass Humphrey and the others for the nomination. Sadly, Robert's life would be cut short by an assassin's bullet right after he clinched the California primary. After being shot at point-blank range by a lone gunman and Palestinian activist named Sirhan Bishara Sirhan, Kennedy was rushed to the hospital. He would die the next day. This devastating blow during an election season was tremendous.

In the immediate aftermath of Kennedy's death, some openly wondered if the Soviets might have somehow been involved. Subsequent interviews with the assassin did not reveal any links with the Kremlin; instead, it showed the psyche of a very troubled man. In fact, he was so troubled that he would make the startling claim that he "blacked out" and did not even remember shooting Kennedy, even though a whole crowd of people saw him do it. Sirhan did not initially give a reason for the attack, but in an interview in 1989, he remarked that he was angry with Robert Kennedy for his professed support of Israel.

The death of Kennedy managed to put Hubert Humphrey in the lead, and he clinched the nomination. But the unrest that Kennedy's assassination generated put the former vice president at a considerable disadvantage. Once it was known that his opponent on the Republican side would be former President Eisenhower's strongman Richard Nixon, Humphrey knew that he was in for a really rough ride. Nixon, citing the terrible unrest in the country, portrayed himself as the "law and order" president, and he appealed to the majority of Americans who weren't out in the street protesting but were simply trying to work and pay the bills to feed their families.

Nixon pledged to this swath of the electorate, whom he dubbed the "silent majority," that he would bring order to the chaos. He also promised that he would bring peace in Vietnam "with honor." It would later be revealed that Hubert Humphrey was getting a little bit of "help" from an unexpected source. It turns out the Soviets preferred the odds of having Hubert Humphrey and the Democrats in the Oval Office than a hardline Republican like Nixon.

As such, the Russians attempted to intervene in President Johnson's last-ditch efforts for a ceasefire with North Vietnam. As strange as it may sound, the Russian government actually pressured their communist allies to meet some of the American demands during peace talks, hoping this would boost President Johnson's successor, Hubert Humphrey, enough to get him elected into office. Yes, as much as recent history has had Americans consider the ramifications of Russian meddling in American elections, such activities have occurred before. They were just another tool in the Soviet toolbox during the Cold War.

Nixon, meanwhile, was in absolute terror that Johnson would manage to get a peace deal with Vietnam before the election. Nixon had been doing well in the polls, but he worried that such a bombshell piece of good fortune for the Democrats might manage to put Hubert Humphrey on top come election day. For Nixon, this was unacceptable. He was the one who would bring "peace with honor" to this Cold War fiasco, not anyone else. This was an October surprise that he just couldn't tolerate.

Fortunately for him, he didn't have to. It was not because North Vietnam pulled out of peace talks, but because the leader of embattled South Vietnam, President Nguyen Van Thieu (*NGUYỄN VĂN THIỆU*), decided to bail out at the last minute. Nixon then went on to win the election in a landslide. But if Richard Nixon had a secret plan to end the Vietnam War, it wasn't readily apparent during his first term in office.

Nixon's main strategy was an arduous one that involved bolstering South Vietnamese forces, training them, and giving them military hardware while slowly withdrawing US troops. This was the so-called "Vietnamization" policy, which basically tried to get the South Vietnamese more involved in the fight and less reliant upon US troops on the ground. Basically, it was a reversal of the buildup that had been created over the years, and this plan was flawed on many levels.

First and foremost, the South Vietnamese, for the most part, had lost the will to fight the North long ago. By this point, they were almost completely reliant on US ground forces, and South Vietnam didn't seem ready to stand on its own any time soon. But even while Nixon was trying to withdraw troops, he ramped up bombings and even sent in more soldiers in nearby Cambodia and Laos in an attempt to cause chaos in the supply lines of the North Vietnamese.

It was around this time that Nixon also perfected what he called his "madman theory." Nixon wanted his overseas communist adversaries to think that he had quite literally gone mad and lost his mind. They wanted them to believe that he was completely unhinged and irrational so that they would be afraid to provoke him lest this crazy "madman" pressed his finger on the button and unleashed a fury of nuclear bombs on them.

It sounds a bit ridiculous, but Nixon believed that he could bluff and bluster his opponents into submission. Nixon described this to Chief of Staff H. R. Haldeman (Nixon just called him Bob).

> I call it the Madman Theory, Bob. I want the North Vietnamese to believe I've reached the point where I might do anything to stop the war. We'll just slip the word to them that, "for God's sake, you know Nixon is obsessed about communism. We can't restrain him when he's angry—and he has his hand on the nuclear button," and Ho Chi Minh himself will be in Paris in two days begging for peace.

Nixon attempted to frighten the Soviet Union in this fashion in 1969 by defying Cold War conventions and engaging in a risky, aggressive practice run with nuclear-armed bombers along the Soviet border. Nixon did this in the hopes that he could pressure the Soviets to change their policy as it pertained to North Vietnam. And although these frightening moves would convince the Soviets to enter into arms control agreements in the coming years, it did virtually nothing in the quest for peace in Vietnam.

The war would drag on throughout the rest of Nixon's first term and into his second. Meanwhile, the North Vietnamese had expanded their aggression to nearby Cambodia. Making the situation even more untenable than it was, Nixon retaliated by sending a joint force of Americans and South Vietnamese into Cambodia in April of 1970. This widening of the war sparked outrage among Americans, and protests naturally occurred.

On May 4th, 1970, a protest at Kent State University in Ohio turned deadly when the National Guard opened fire on protesters, killing four students. This incident prompted singer-songwriter Neil Young to write his infamous protest song called "Ohio." The song, which was performed by Crosby, Stills, Nash & Young, lambasts the Nixon administration. Neil wrote the lyrics, "Tin soldiers and Nixon's coming! / We're finally on our own! / This summer I hear the drumming. / Four dead in Ohio!"

Despite these criticisms, the offensives continued over the next couple of years. By 1972, Nixon had embarked upon a new strategy: a charm offensive aimed at North Vietnam's benefactors. Most notably, Richard Nixon managed to engage in high-level talks with China in what would become known as Nixon's great Cold War "détente." President Nixon's visit to China can't be underestimated. The fact that the leader of communist China would openly speak with an American president shook up the entire calculus of the Cold War. This was the first time that an American head of state recognized the Chinese communist government, let alone sat down for a discussion.

Nixon, ever the strategist, was well aware that a wedge had been driven between the Soviets and the Chinese, and he was ready to exploit it for all it was worth. President Nixon further realized that it was the Soviets who were supporting the North Vietnamese at this point, not the Chinese government. Nixon was hoping to court China so that he could gain additional leverage when negotiating an end to the Vietnam War.

For his part, communist Chinese leader Mao Zedong welcomed the opportunity to have a bargaining chip of his own to use against the Soviets. Zedong, who was determined to strike a different path for communist China than the one taken by Soviet Russia, also welcomed the prospects of trade with the United States. Nixon's trip to China marked the very beginning of modern US-China relations and established the framework upon which that relationship was built. Even though it didn't achieve much when it came to ending the war in Vietnam, the dialogue that Nixon established was a phenomenal achievement in itself.

Meanwhile, the North Vietnamese were on the march. In late March of 1972, they launched their infamous Easter Offensive, also known as the Nguyen Hue Offensive, which threatened to completely knock out the South Vietnamese forces. Nixon couldn't tolerate such an ignoble defeat, so he launched Operation Linebacker, which utilized a massive bombing campaign against North Vietnam. The American offensive successfully pushed the North Vietnamese back (just like a linebacker would in a football game) to their side of the DMZ.

The Vietnam War was once again a stalemate, but this show of force and resolve on the part of Nixon finally convinced the Soviets to consider brokering a peace deal in Vietnam. It happened to be another election year in 1972, and Nixon was struggling to get a peace deal worked out before voters cast their ballot on November

7th. But, once again, South Vietnam President Nguyen Van Thieu spoiled these efforts, backing out at the last minute.

As it turned out, Nixon didn't have much to worry about as it pertained to his reelection, as he won by an even greater margin than he did the first time. Nixon absolutely pummeled Senator George McGovern in the popular vote and won just about every state in the Union (Nixon won forty-nine out of fifty states). Considering the fact that Nixon was eventually forced to resign in disgrace, it is quite amazing to realize just how many people actually voted to put him back into office.

At any rate, after Nixon gained a second term, the talks between North and South Vietnam continued to go nowhere. Wishing to force the North's hand, Nixon engaged in a massive bombing run on December 14th, which was known as the "Christmas Bombings" (its more formal name was Operation Linebacker II). Negotiations once again took center stage the following January, and on January 27th, 1973, a tentative agreement was made between the two parties.

But back home, all hell was about to break loose for Nixon when the Watergate scandal broke later that year. It was discovered that Nixon, who so handily won the election, had been sending operatives to spy on the Democrats. Not only that, but they had actually broken into the Democratic headquarters in Washington, DC. An investigation ensued, which eventually led back to Nixon himself. Nixon was caught red-handed, and he was likely to be impeached and ultimately removed from office. Knowing that Nixon was doomed, his colleagues convinced him to resign.

Without Nixon at the helm, the North Vietnamese were emboldened to toss any previous agreements made to the side. In 1975, they marched right into Saigon and ended the war not through peace but through an outright communist takeover. This ended the existence of South Vietnam, as Vietnam was united under one communist ideology. This hard-fought battle in America's Cold War with the Soviet Union had been lost. Cold

War warrior Richard Milhous Nixon, meanwhile, was left to retire in obscurity.

Just a year after his resignation, Nixon nearly died in August of 1974 when he was rushed to the hospital, suffering from a pulmonary embolism. This event apparently inspired the aforementioned singer-songwriter and Nixon antagonist Neil Young to write up a piece to capture this moment. Young proved to be an interesting character in Nixon's life. As much as he criticized Nixon in the protest song "Ohio," Young wrote a musical take on Nixon called "Campaigner," which had a much more sympathetic tone.

Reflecting on Nixon's frailty, Neil Young hauntingly sang, "Hospitals have made him cry / But there's always a freeway in his eye / Though his beach just got too crowded for his stroll / Roads stretch out like healthy veins / And wild gift horses strain the reins / Where even Richard Nixon has got soul / Even Richard Nixon has got soul."

Nixon was probably the most vilified person on the planet at this point, yet in his somber, plaintive singing voice, Neil wanted to step in and remind us that Nixon wasn't a monster. He was only human. He struggled and toiled just like anyone else, and no matter what he may have done in the past, even the hardline anti-communist Cold War warrior Richard Nixon had a soul.

Chapter 6 – An East African Cold War

"I'm a military man, I did what I did only because my country had to be saved from tribalism and feudalism. If I failed, it was only because I was betrayed. The so-called genocide was nothing more than just a war in defense of the revolution and a system from which all have benefited."

-Mengistu Haile Mariam

The African continent is often omitted in discussions of the impact of the Cold War, but the Cold War had its impact here all the same. The chill of the Cold War was felt the most keenly in East Africa. Somalia, the nation now almost uniquely synonymous with war and instability, became a communist state in 1969 when a Somali general named Mohamed Siad Barre seized power.

At first, Siad Barre was the darling of the Soviet Union and was showered with unconditional aid. But when one of Somalia's traditional rivals in the Horn of Africa, Ethiopia, flipped to communism as well, tension was in the air. Ethiopia is an ancient country, and it is the only African nation to have never been conquered by a foreign power. The Italians tried to take over Ethiopia on two separate occasions and failed both times.

Ethiopia has a long history, which boasts a lengthy line of Ethiopian monarchs referred to as "emperors." These Ethiopian kings are said to trace their lineage all the way back to the Queen of Sheba, who is famously said to have visited Israel's King Solomon sometime around 959 BCE. According to legend, the two became quite close. Close enough, in fact, to produce a son whom the Ethiopians called Menelik (not to be confused with Menelik II, who famously drove the Italians out of Ethiopia in 1898). Menelik would become the emperor of the Ethiopian domain, and through him, a long line of kings would reign over Ethiopia over the next several centuries.

All of this would come to an end when the last Ethiopian emperor, Haile Selassie, was taken down by a communist coup in 1974. Selassie, who had reigned over Ethiopia since the 1930s and steered his country through the fascist aggression of Italy's Benito Mussolini during World War II, was taken down by a Marxist-Leninist group known as the Derg.

At first, the emperor was placed under house arrest, but the Derg showed its teeth in 1975 by executing the emperor. Selassie was ultimately replaced by a low-ranking soldier and Derg member by the name of Mengistu Haile Mariam. Before the communist takeover, Ethiopia was a strong ally of the United States. America had entrusted this African constitutional monarchy to stand as a bulwark against communism, especially the threat of communist Somalia.

But as soon as Ethiopia transformed into a communist state, America cut off its relations with its former friend and partner in the region. The Soviet Union, of course, wholeheartedly embraced Ethiopia, hoping that it would be a valuable chess piece for them in the region of East Africa. Now that both Somalia and Ethiopia were communist, the Soviets hoped these two nations could develop solidarity with each other. But Somalia's Siad Barre apparently didn't see it that way. He was eager to expand his own territory, and he shocked his Soviet backers when he ordered his troops to invade Ethiopia's Ogaden region in 1977. Ogaden is a disputed territory that lies just west of Somalia's borders and contains a sizeable population of ethnic Somalis.

With these developments, the Soviets now had a communist country fighting another communist country in East Africa. This was certainly not what the Soviets had anticipated. Which one would they back? The Soviets were angered by the Somali invasion and furthermore valued Ethiopia as the greater prize, so they decided to scale back support for Somalia and back Ethiopia instead.

This move absolutely infuriated Somali leader Siad Barre. So much so that in November of 1977, he sent all Soviet personnel in Somalia packing. This was perhaps a good thing for Ethiopia, as the country needed the Soviet Union's help. The revolution that had brought the communists to power had left much of Ethiopia in a fractured state. The Ethiopian military was not quite prepared for a war with Somalia. But after the Soviets dropped some billion dollars' worth of military equipment and transported tens of thousands of Cuban fighters, courtesy of Fidel Castro, the Ethiopians were ready to fight.

The Ethiopians and their allies devastated the Somali army and drove them out of Ethiopia. Somalia was forced to recognize Ethiopia's right to Ogaden and gave up any future plans to contest Ethiopia's dominance in the region. These developments put the United States in a very strange position. During the Cold War, whenever the Soviets supported any one side during a conflict, the United States, almost by default, would end up supporting the other. But Somalia was a communist country. How could the United States aid communists? Despite the ideological challenge of aiding communists, if it could help thwart the Soviets in the region, the United States decided it would be worth their while to aid Somalia.

Somalia was also of strategic interest to the Americans since it was located so close to the Middle East and, in particular, the Persian Gulf. For this reason, the United States worked out a deal in which they offered up much-needed aid to the Somalis in exchange for access to Somalia's ports and airbases in Mogadishu, Chisimayu (Kismayo), and Berbera. In Ethiopia, the communist leadership of Mengistu was continuing to shore up his support from the Soviet Union, receiving billions of dollars in aid throughout the whole war effort.

Despite this support, Ethiopia was having a hard time getting up off the ground. Terrible famines struck the land in the 1980s. It was one of these famines that actually inspired the historic Live Aid concert, which had several notable celebrities singing "We Are the World" while they did their best to raise money for the cause. It's debatable how much of this money actually helped starving children and how much went into Mengistu's pockets, but the pop culture attention did help shine a spotlight on a country that was suffering as a result of the Cold War.

It is rather ironic that Mengistu, who had promised prosperity to the Ethiopian proletariat, often failed to provide basic sustenance to his own people. Mengistu rose to power on the popular slogan "Land to the Tiller." This meant that land from aristocratic Ethiopians would be divvied up and redistributed to Ethiopian farmhands. Yet this system of distribution was so disruptive that it affected the entire agricultural sector, causing widespread famine.

Supposedly in order to combat the famine that was rocking his country, Mengistu began to relocate Ethiopians from the "arid northern provinces" in the mountains to farmlands in the south in the mid-1980s. Ethiopians in these northern regions were hit particularly hard by the famine. This move would supposedly both provide labor for the farms and provide relief to those who were suffering the most.

Each Ethiopian sent south was promised their own plot of land, and "cattle, seed, fertilizer, and medical assistance for at least one year." This ill-advised relocation effort would uproot nearly two million Ethiopians. The Western world, which had already borne witness to Mengistu's communist regime redistributing Western aid for famine to his own military, was highly skeptical, to say the least.

An ulterior motive on Mengistu's part would later be uncovered. People eventually realized that most of the Ethiopians that Mengistu had relocated from those "arid northern provinces" were from locales that had been actively resisting his authority. So, it would seem, that the relocation of this entire population was partially a scheme to disrupt an outburst of popular resentment against his regime.

However, by 1991, neither the help of the Soviet Union nor countless American celebrities singing "We Are the World" could stave off the collapse of Mengistu Haile Mariam's doomed communist regime. A new popular revolution had risen up in northern Ethiopia in the region of Tigray—one of the very regions that Mengistu had been trying hard to suppress. Mengistu was ultimately ousted by a popular Tigray leader, Meles Zenawi, who was backed by the TPLF (Tigray People's Liberation Front).

No matter how much Mengistu and his Marxists tried to shove communism down the throats of the average Ethiopian, their ideology was always at odds with the general public. Some believed the land reform was necessary in order to uplift the peasant class, but other aspects of communism never fit well in Ethiopian society.

For one thing, Ethiopia is a deeply religious land. Ethiopia has links to Judaism in the Old Testament, and it was one of the first nations to become Christian by the time of the New Testament. The deep roots of the Ethiopian Orthodox Tewahedo Church, which date back to around 300 CE, were not going to be uprooted so easily by the godless communists.

Meles Zenawi would have the full support of the Ethiopian Orthodox Church in his mission to drive the communists out of the country. By the time Meles Zenawi and his freedom fighters made their way to the Ethiopian capital of Addis Ababa, they were allowed to enter "virtually unopposed," demonstrating the extreme level of disdain the nation had for Mengistu. Mengistu ended up fleeing to Zimbabwe in May of 1991, and Soviet aid and communication were cut off shortly thereafter.

Even while Mengistu's regime was falling apart, Americans began pulling out of Somalia, as the regime of Siad Barre was disintegrating. Somalia's post-Cold War fate would be far less fortunate than that of Ethiopia's. While Ethiopia made the transition from a communist state to a federal republic, Somalia went from communism to utter chaos and anarchy—a state of persistent turmoil that Somalis are still trying to find their way out of. It's a tale of two East African countries affected by one ever-pervasive Cold War.

Chapter 7 – Cold War Secrets and a Place Called Area 51

"Even during the years of the Cold War, the intense confrontation between the Soviet Union and the United States, we always avoided any direct clash between our civilians and, most certainly, between our military."

-Vladimir Putin

As the Cold War intensified, so did the secrecy on both sides. This was especially the case when it came to the development of new military hardware. In the United States, as the Cold War loomed with widespread fear of Soviet espionage, these fears led to the desire to have a top-secret facility where US engineers could work on the latest high-tech wizardry free from distraction and unwanted attention. For this reason, a remote stretch of Nevada desert that had been labeled by the US military as nothing more than "Area 51" became appealing.

Prior to becoming a proving ground for military tech, Area 51 was known as the Nevada Test Site. Shortly after World War II, this desolate desert range was used to test nuclear bombs. With the onset of the Cold War, the Air Force and CIA became more heavily involved and began operating out of a region within Area 51 called Groom Lake. In 1955, at Groom Lake, the CIA launched a special project called AQUATONE. Project AQUATONE was an effort to create a spy plane that could fly over Soviet airspace and not be detected by the Soviet Union.

This was still a couple of years before Sputnik, and spy satellites had not yet been developed. Back in those days, the only real way to gather intelligence on your enemy was to simply violate their airspace and fly right over. Of course, if US airmen were caught doing such a thing, they were not only at risk of being shot down but also of kicking off a wider conflict with the Soviet Union itself. No country wants its airspace to be violated after all, and it would have been fully within its rights to take proactive measures.

Nevertheless, US officials just had to know what the Soviets were up to, and the only way they could keep tabs on their enemy was to have a plane that could successfully penetrate Soviet defenses, snap a few photos of what was happening on the ground, and come back undetected. This was what Project AQUATONE was all about, and it was up to the engineers at Groom Lake to design an aircraft that could meet these specifications. US intelligence already had a good idea of what Soviet air defenses consisted of, and they knew that Soviet radars had a limited range of functionality.

It was realized that if they could simply create a plane that could fly high enough, it would not be detected from Soviet radar systems. It was in the quest for this high-altitude vehicle that the U-2 spy plane was born. The developers of the U-2 were determined to create a plane that could rise above 70,000 feet so it could breach Soviet airspace without being detected. The engineers at Area 51 rapidly rushed out their first model of this craft in the summer of 1955.

Once production had commenced, the US military took a backseat operationally speaking and had CIA agents pilot the craft rather than service members. Just in case the U-2 went down, it was considered prudent to have a CIA pilot in regular dress rather than a soldier in army fatigues. This was done so that the army could deny involvement. It's important to note that the U-2 was never made to appear like a military craft. In fact, the first few to roll off the assembly line were outfitted with the "NACA" logo. NACA, which stands for National Advisory Committee for Aeronautics, was a flight research group founded in 1915 that would later become the more familiar NASA. If the U-2 ever had to make an emergency landing somewhere, the CIA had a cover story ready just in case. If spotted, they would claim that the U-2 was a research craft studying meteorological phenomena in the upper atmosphere. In reality, the main purpose of the U-2 was to spy on the Soviet Union.

The U-2 would successfully conduct spying missions over Soviet airspace for the next few years, providing valuable intelligence on things such as troop positions in Eastern Europe and missile sites in Russia. One of the most important things the U-2 spy plane revealed was that there was a major discrepancy between what Soviet leader Nikita Khrushchev claimed to have as it pertained to nuclear missiles and what was actually on the ground. To the great relief of the Eisenhower administration, it was discovered that Khrushchev was bluffing, as the Soviet stockpile was actually much smaller than what Khrushchev had claimed.

The radar systems of the Soviet Union were actually more sophisticated than US planners had anticipated, and they were indeed able to detect these flyovers. But even so, the Soviets, at the time, had no plane or missile that could fly high enough to intercept the American craft. In 1960, that all changed when the Soviets came up with a surface-to-air missile (SAM) that could finally reach the high-flying U-2.

This capability was then proven to the world on May 1ˢᵗ, 1960. A thirty-year-old pilot by the name of Gary Powers was targeted by the Soviet's new SAM. Gary was flying along, snapping photos of Soviet installations like usual. Since he had an altitude of 70,000 feet, he believed he was safely out of range of the Soviets. His peace of mind was shattered when an explosion suddenly rocked his plane. The source of the blast was a SAM that had exploded just underneath the U-2. Although this missile didn't hit the plane directly, its shockwaves caused the U-2 to drop down to a lower altitude.

Once that happened, the Soviets locked onto Gary's craft again and sent another SAM racing right toward him. This one found its target. The blast ripped the U-2's wings right off and sent what was left of Gary's plane into a nosedive. Since his craft flew so high in the atmosphere, Gary wore a pressurized suit—a kind of predecessor to what the astronauts would later wear. Since pressure in the craft was lost, the suit began to fill up to compensate, which made it hard for Gary to toggle his controls.

Initially, he considered pressing the ejection button to send his seat flying out of the craft, just as he had trained. But Gary had been knocked forward in the cockpit to such an extent that he knew if he pressed that button, his legs would collide with the "canopy rails" of the craft, most likely severing them from his body. So while his plane was violently tumbling down to the ground, Gary made the decision to simply open the cockpit of the craft and jump out. Incredibly enough, from this high altitude, Gary was able to gently drop down to Earth unscathed as his parachute deployed.

This would have been a remarkable feat, one that might have otherwise been celebrated had it not been for the fact Gary was making an emergency landing. He was, of course, knee-deep in enemy territory, and once his feet touched Soviet soil, there would be no easy way out. Gary was immediately discovered by Soviet ground forces and taken into custody. It took a while to find someone who spoke English well enough, but as soon as they did, the interrogation began.

They asked many questions, and one of them was about the secret "desert base" in Nevada that Powers had flown from. They wanted to know about Area 51. Yes, the Soviets had been tracking the American spy craft that had originated from this remote section of Nevada, and they knew that it was the site of the mysterious spy plane's development. However, Gary would not divulge any knowledge about Area 51 and instead claimed that he had flown out of California.

Gary initially stuck to the rehearsed story that he was simply conducting meteorological research and had been blown off course. But when it was obvious that his Soviet handlers were not going to believe him, he finally admitted that he was on a spying mission for the CIA. Initially, the Americans were completely in the dark as to what may have happened to their missing pilot. About a week after Gary's capture, the mystery was solved when Soviet leader Nikita Khrushchev announced to the world that they had an American spy plane and its pilot in their possession.

This was a huge embarrassment to President Eisenhower, and it forced him to eventually admit that the US was indeed conducting surveillance on the Soviet Union. Gary Powers was put on trial in August of 1960, and he was sentenced to ten years for his trespasses. Fortunately for Gary, he would eventually be bailed out by his American handlers when a "spy swap" was carried out between the two Cold War camps in 1962. Powers was returned to the Americans in exchange for the Soviet spy Rudolf Abel.

The failure of the U-2 was devastating, and it caused the folks back at Area 51 to go back to the drawing board once again in search of a plane that would not be detected by the Soviet Union. It was shortly after the U-2 debacle that the folks at Groom Lake began working on what would become known as the SR-71 "Blackbird." This was truly an advanced craft, and it looked like something straight out of *Buck Rogers*. The final product would also have tremendous capability, as it was able to fly 20,000 feet higher than the U-2, all the way to the outer atmosphere of the planet.

The Blackbird isn't exactly a spaceplane, but it comes close. It remains the highest-flying air-breathing engine craft in existence. The Blackbird is also fast, with a top speed of about 2,200 mph. This craft wouldn't have the same problem that Gary Powers encountered because if a missile was launched in its direction, it could simply take evasive action and outfly it! But perhaps most importantly, the sleek design of the craft significantly reduced its radar cross-section (the measure of how detectable an aircraft is by radar).

To be clear, the Blackbird is not a stealth aircraft, but it's certainly a forerunner. The Blackbird would go on to engage in several reconnaissance missions during the Vietnam War, always staying one step ahead of enemy air defenses. It's estimated that the North Vietnamese launched some 800 surface-to-air missiles at Blackbirds during the course of the war, but this proved to be an exercise in futility, for this nimble craft was able to evade them every time.

The greatest threat that a pilot faced when flying the Blackbird was technical failures of their own equipment. Just such a technical difficulty occurred in 1987 when an SR-71, which was sent to take a look at Soviet installations along the Baltic coast, had one of its engines suddenly explode. This caused the plane to lose altitude, and the pilot was immediately forced to attempt an emergency landing. The closest friendly location within reach was Sweden. The craft headed into Swedish airspace and was intercepted by the Swedish air force. Upon identifying the plane, the Swedes escorted the craft over to Denmark.

This escort would prove critical to the Blackbird's mission since it would later be revealed that the plane had been spotted by Russian warplanes. At one point, a Russian MiG-25 had actually locked onto the craft and was prepared to shoot it down. But once the Swedes intervened, the Russians backed down, not willing to risk hitting the Swedish aircraft, allowing the Blackbird to be successfully escorted back to safety.

By the late 1980s, the Pentagon was considering the retirement of the Blackbird, but there was already a replacement in the works. The folks at Area 51 had been working hard to perfect something they sarcastically called the "hopeless diamond." The "hopeless diamond" was in reference to the new stealth aircrafts' "diamond-shaped cross section," which could deflect ground-based radar systems. Engineers knew this diamond shape was crucial to deflecting enemy radar, but they also knew that it was extremely difficult to make a diamond-shaped craft able to fly.

The first prototype of what would become a stealth fighter plane was called the Have Blue, and it was rolled off the assembly line in the late 1970s. The engineers may have felt it was hopeless, but they kept hammering away at the design until they were able to make a revolutionary aircraft, one with a diamond-shaped cross-section, swept wings, and inward-canted vertical stabilizers. The end result looked like something out of this world. And the general public agreed. Sightings of this classified craft often generated UFO (unidentified flying object) reports.

In 1988, it would be revealed to the world that the new F-117 Nighthawk, a stealth fighter plane, was not a visitor from another planet but rather a highly sophisticated next-generation aircraft. Now declassified, the craft would go on to see its first major bit of action in 1991 during the Gulf War. The stealth aircraft were able to penetrate Iraqi airspace with impunity, leading Saddam Hussein to have his air defenses fire wildly into the air, hoping to hit the craft at random. However, the stealth craft proved impervious during this engagement.

With the help of the stealth craft, the United States ruled the air over Iraq and quickly shut the forces of Saddam Hussein down. The Soviets couldn't help but notice, and they began to feel the squeeze even more. The Soviet Union had already been struggling to keep up with American military advances, using about a quarter of their GDP (gross domestic product) to do so, but now they had simply been outdone. They had no aircraft that could compete with these stealth fighters. And even though the American planes were targeting Iraq, they might as well have been launched against the Soviets since this awesome display of American know-how and might made many in Russia aware that the Cold War was all but lost.

Previously, the Russians had been intimidated by Ronald Reagan's claims of having SDI (Strategic Defensive Initiative) weapons in space that could deflect nuclear weapons. History would prove this to be more of a bluff than reality, but with the stealth fighters, the world had indisputable proof of a major advance in military development. And it was one that the increasingly weakened Soviet Union would have no way of keeping up with. Although it wasn't the only factor involved, the revelation of this Cold War secret helped to hasten the end of the Cold War. The Soviet Union would ultimately collapse before 1991 was over.

Chapter 8 – Soviets, Afghanistan, and a Little Bit of SALT

"During the Cold War, America undertook serious military cuts only once: after the election of Richard Nixon, during the Vietnam War. The result: Vietnam fell to the communists, the Russians moved into Afghanistan, and American influence around the globe waned dramatically."

-Ben Shapiro

At the start of the Cold War, both the United States and the Soviet Union began to build up their nuclear arms at an alarming rate. The United States—the first country on the planet to develop nuclear weapons—initially had the edge, but the Soviet Union caught up quickly. The Soviets developed their first atomic bomb in 1949 and then went on to test its first hydrogen bomb in 1955.

There's sometimes a little bit of confusion over the difference between things like an atomic bomb and a hydrogen bomb, so let me explain. They are both nuclear bombs, but a hydrogen bomb is much more powerful than an atomic bomb. Atomic bombs were the first nuclear bombs ever created, so it makes sense they aren't as powerful as hydrogen ones. However, even atomic bombs have the capability of massive destruction; look at the atomic bombs dropped on Japan, which were powerful enough to incinerate whole cities and take thousands of lives, both upon impact and due to its aftereffects.

At its most basic definition, a nuclear weapon is a bomb that "derives its destructive force" from nuclear reactions. Atomic bombs achieve this by splitting the atom, while hydrogen bombs rely on even more powerful fusion reactions of hydrogen. Until the advent of the intercontinental ballistic missiles in the late 1950s, these weapons had to be dropped from planes. With ICBMs, a nuclear-tipped missile could be launched with the push of a button.

Since both the Soviet Union and the United States stockpiled ICBMs, both countries developed the ability to destroy each other in a status quo known as mutually assured destruction. If one country unloaded its nuclear missiles, the other was sure to follow suit, and they would both be destroyed in the process. This mutually assured destruction was felt to be the ultimate check, as it would make sure that neither side used their weapons.

Even so, the arms race grew dangerously out of control. Eventually, both sides began to grow anxious over the enormous amount of nuclear weaponry they had and sought to reduce them. It was this mutual desire for reduction that led to SALT (Strategic Arms Limitation Talks). The first SALT agreement, SALT I, was reached on May 26th, 1972. This agreement stipulated that both parties would put a freeze on "the number of strategic ballistic missile launchers" each country had, as well as putting a limit on the range of ICBMs.

This was a breakthrough deal, and it was hoped that there would be more to come. The next SALT treaty, SALT II, came about in the summer of 1979 under the stewardship of American President Jimmy Carter and Soviet Premier Leonid Brezhnev. This treaty was more comprehensive than the last. It stated that both sides should reduce their "strategic forces" down to 2,250 each. However, these plans would come into peril when the Soviet Union invaded Afghanistan six months later.

Soviet forces poured into Afghanistan on Christmas Eve, December 24th, 1979. The reason? To support Afghanistan's fledgling communist party. Afghanistan had

experienced a pseudo-revolution in 1978 known as the Saur Revolution. This put a small local group of Afghan communists in power to the great displeasure of much of the rest of the nation. When those dissatisfied Afghans tried to remove the communists, the Soviets used it as an excuse to invade the country outright.

The Soviet invasion and occupation earned an immediate rebuke from the United States, with President Jimmy Carter denouncing the actions and cutting all ties with the Soviets. This officially put an end to détente, the period of reduced tensions between the two major parties of the Cold War. Carter was so incensed that he even had the United States boycott the Olympic Games in 1980. He also asked the Senate to consider suspending SALT II.

And the Americans weren't the only ones denouncing the Soviet Union for their intervention in Afghanistan. China denounced the Russians as well. The Sino-Soviet split had long been underway, and the two communist countries had already had some pretty volatile differences in the past. China was now making its displeasure known by actively supporting the Mujahideen fighters on the ground in a bid to help thwart the efforts of the Russians.

China didn't like the Soviet invasion for a number of reasons, but probably what irked them the most was how close the conflict was to home. Afghanistan is in the proximity of northwestern China, and operations taking place there would not go unnoticed by the Chinese. In order to project strength to the encroaching Russians, China openly mobilized its armed forces on its northwestern frontlines, in China's Xinjiang region.

Nevertheless, despite this backlash, the Soviets were not deterred enough to leave Afghanistan. They would end up staying in the country for ten long, bloody years, during which they fought off endless waves of Afghan insurgencies waged by an Islamic group known as the Mujahideen. In many ways, this Cold War flashpoint provided the United States, which had lost so much blood and money through Soviet-backed Vietnamese aggressions, a chance to get a little revenge on their Cold War adversary.

It sounds rather capricious to present this situation in such terms, but the Cold War, by and large, was very much a tit for tat type of exchange. And US officials began to openly talk about how Afghanistan was going to be the Soviet's Vietnam. A secret order via President Jimmy Carter read, "Our ultimate goal is the withdrawal of Soviet troops from Afghanistan. Even if this is not attainable, we should make Soviet involvement as costly as possible."

The CIA began to immediately sponsor and establish Afghan rebel groups, providing them with arms, training, and intelligence. But the greatest breakthrough was when the US delivered the Afghans a shoulder-fired rocket launcher known as a "Stinger." Stingers were heat-seeking missiles that could knock Russian craft right out of the air. Until this advance, the Russians dominated Afghanistan's skies. The Russians, of course, knew these new weapons were from the United States, but they weren't going to press any further about it. Instead, they simply took the abuse, and Afghans repeatedly knocked Russian helicopters and aircraft out of the air.

Finally, the Russians had enough and pulled out of Afghanistan in 1989, but they left a tremendous vacuum in their wake. As soon as the Russians left, the rebels—many of them American-trained fighters—began to battle for power. It was out of this chaotic storm that groups like Al-Qaeda came to prominence.

Al-Qaeda was tied to the aforementioned Mujahideen, which was a jihadist resistance movement against the Soviets, of which none other than future terrorist mastermind Osama bin Laden was a part. Bin Laden would later go on to head Al-Qaeda. Since Al-Qaeda has its roots in the Mujahideen, in some ways, you could logically conclude that the CIA had a part in founding Al-Qaeda, as they were the ones that helped these rebels gain a foothold against the Russians. This means that the US inadvertently trained what would later become a terrorist group. Both Jimmy Carter and Ronald Reagan wanted to make the Soviets suffer after they invaded Afghanistan, but the repercussions would last for decades.

Chapter 9 – Ronald Reagan and the Evil Empire

"Overcoming the Cold War required courage from the people of Central and Eastern Europe and what was then the German Democratic Republic, but it also required the steadfastness of Western partner over many decades when many had long lost hope of integration of the two Germanys and Europe."

-Angela Merkel

Ronald Reagan was a hardliner when it came to the war against communism. When he first ran for president in the 1980 election, he made it perfectly clear that he wanted to put an end to what he called the "Vietnam Syndrome." This was the notion that the tragic and ill-fated Vietnam War had created a defeatist kind of attitude among Americans; Reagan believed these feelings of defeatism needed to be rooted out.

This often led him to use bellicose and harsh language toward the Soviet Union. This was a stance that some of his critics felt was unnecessarily—and perhaps dangerously—aggressive. At the same time, during his debut press conference on January 29th, 1981, Reagan seemed ready to extend the olive branch if the possibility presented itself. He stated his openness toward "an actual reduction in the numbers of nuclear weapons."

Reagan also made clear his view that the Soviets would stop at nothing to dominate the globe. Reagan declared that "their goal must be the promotion of world revolution and a one-world Socialist or Communist state." And if one were to brush up on the teachings of Marx or Lenin, you would indeed find their words rife with just such a sentiment. A utopian vision of a worldwide communist government has never been far from any budding communist's lips.

With these words, Ronald Reagan drew a line in the sand and made his position clear. But perhaps the most powerful thing gleaned from Reagan's first press conference wasn't his views but rather his perception of how the Soviets viewed the world. Reagan went on to claim that the Soviet Union would stop at nothing to obtain world domination. Reagan remarked, "Now, as long as they do that and as long as they, at the same time, have openly and publicly declared that the only morality they recognize is what will further their cause, meaning they reserve unto themselves the right to commit any crime, to lie, to cheat, in order to attain that, and that is moral, not immoral, and we operate on a different set of standards, I think when you do business with them, even at a détente, you keep that in mind."

From the very beginning of his administration, President Ronald Reagan made it clear that his approach to the Cold War would not be business as usual. He felt that the years of détente in the 1970s had not provided any substantial return for the effort that the United States put in. Now that he was at the helm, he was determined to change the direction that the country was heading in. It wasn't that Reagan didn't value peace or past agreements with the Soviets such as SALT; he simply felt that the Russians had violated the terms of these treaties so many times that they just weren't worth the trouble of upholding anymore.

So instead of seeking to ease the Cold War through an arms control détente, Reagan instead sought to up the stakes. At this point, he began to set in motion a plan to beat the Soviets at their own game. Instead of arms control, he would increase US military expenditures and dare the Soviets to keep up. So it was that Reagan went where former President Jimmy Carter feared to tread; he increased the US arsenal with things like neutron bombs and allocated production for more B-1 bombers.

Reagan, although he was elected by a clear majority of the American public, generated much fear and anxiety in those who opposed him. They feared that the president's hardline stance would lead to nuclear war with the Soviet Union. Due to this political polarization and animosity against Reagan, some began to fear for his personal safety. Those fears were subsequently realized in a terrible way on March 30th, 1981, when Reagan was shot by a would-be assassin just outside of a Hilton Hotel in Washington, DC.

He had just finished giving a speech at the Hilton and was being escorted to the limousine that would take him to his next destination when a deranged gunman by the name of John Hinckley Jr. ambushed Reagan and his entourage and opened fire. In this exchange, Reagan, as well as his press secretary James Brady, were struck. Brady got the worst of it, getting hit in the head. Reagan was actually struck by a bullet that ricocheted off the limousine. It hit him under his left arm, with the bullet piercing through his lungs. Secret service agent Timothy McCarthy and police officer Thomas Delahanty were also wounded that day.

As soon as the gunfire erupted, Reagan was pushed into the car and rushed to the hospital. If it wasn't for this quick and decisive action, he very well could have died that day. Although Reagan had not received a direct hit, the fact that his lung was pierced led to severe internal bleeding, and he was said to have been "close to death" when he was brought to George Washington University Hospital. Reagan was stabilized, and he made a dramatic recovery.

Upon his return to the White House, there was a great outpouring of sympathy for Reagan, and even his detractors began to warm up to him. Feeling that he had been given a rare second chance, Reagan believed that he had a mandate to do something really great. In many ways, he felt that providence had placed upon him the mission for ending the Cold War. Furthermore, in the immediate attempt, some even wondered if the Soviets were behind the assassination attempt.

However, it was rather quickly realized that the assassin, John Hinckley Jr., was simply a very troubled individual. Hinckley had apparently been infatuated with actress Jodie Foster and thought that killing the president would impress her. If this sounds like the ramblings of a madman, it's because Hinckley was criminally insane. He would end up spending over the next thirty years in a mental intuition for what he had done. He was eventually released in 2016, as he was ruled to be no longer a menace to society.

At any rate, after the Americans ruled out Soviet intervention in the hit on Reagan, President Reagan began to think of personally reaching out to his Soviet counterpart. He actually went so far as to write a personal letter to Leonid Brezhnev, but he was convinced by his secretary, Alexander Haig, that this might "send the wrong signal." The Soviets, after all, were engaging full force in their aggression in Afghanistan, and if Reagan wanted to project strength, the time wasn't exactly ripe for the extension of an olive branch.

Instead, Haig had an official memorandum typed up. While it highlighted some positive developments as it pertained to the Soviet Union, such as an end to the grain embargo that had hurt the Soviet economy, it firmly addressed issues of concern for America, such as the Soviet invasion of Afghanistan. In addition to this main piece of correspondence, Reagan's personal letter was ultimately also included. The letter beseeched Brezhnev to consider "the very real, everyday problems of the people" that each man mutually represented. It was an attempt to break through the Cold War ice with personal warmth and empathy for the average citizen who lived on each side of the Iron Curtain.

Only the policy-driven letter got a response from the Soviets, who roundly rejected all of the points that the Reagan administration had made. Rebuffed as he was, Reagan was now truly ready to play hardball with the Soviets. And in doing so, he had the cautious and circumspect Haig replaced by the more hawkish George Shultz. Shultz became Reagan's new secretary of state in the summer of 1982, and from that point forward, Reagan once again assumed a much more adversarial stance against the Soviet Union.

Around this time, Reagan made one of his most famous declarations in regard to how he envisioned the end of the Cold War would take shape. During a visit to England, he famously declared that it was "the march of freedom and democracy which will leave Marxism-Leninism on the ash-heap of history as it has left other tyrannies which stifle the freedom and muzzle the self-expression of the people." By the following year of 1983, he was openly calling the Soviet Union an "Evil Empire."

This tough talk alarmed a good segment of the skittish public, who feared that Reagan's saber-rattling could lead to a nuclear exchange between the two superpowers. This led to several anti-war protests breaking out in both the United States and Europe during Reagan's first term. Reagan's own daughter Patti took part in these protests.

But as tumultuous as Reagan's Cold War strategy might have seemed at the time, Reagan knew what he was doing. He outlined his goals in National Security Decision Directive 75. The directive's stated objectives were the following.

> To contain and over time reverse Soviet expansionism by competing effectively on a sustained basis with the Soviet Union in all international arenas—particularly in the overall

military balance and geographical regions of priority concern to the United States. This will remain the primary focus of U.S. policy toward the USSR. To promote, within the narrow limits available to us, the process of change in the Soviet Union toward a more pluralistic political and economic system in which the power of the privileged ruling elite is gradually reduced. The U.S. recognizes that Soviet aggressiveness has deep roots in the internal system, and that relations with the USSR should therefore take into account whether or not they help to strengthen this system and its capacity to engage in aggression. To engage the Soviet Union in negotiations to attempt to reach agreements which protect and enhance U.S. interests and which are consistent with the principle of strict reciprocity and mutual interest. This is important when the Soviet Union is in the midst of a process of political succession.

Shortly after this directive went out, Secretary of State Shultz sent out a memorandum that pertained to US-Soviet relations in 1983. This document "called for countering the new Soviet activism by starting an intensified dialogue with Moscow." This dialogue was supposed to focus on "realism and mutual interests." This was Reagan's "real-politick" in action, in which he would try to engage with the Soviets directly in a pragmatic fashion to see what common ground could be gained.

His first point of contact was a Soviet ambassador named Anatoly Dobrynin. This line of communication was believed to be vital, and on June 15th, 1983, Shultz himself stated as much when he declared the following before Congress: "In the past two years this nation...has made a fundamental commitment to restoring its military and economic power and moral and spiritual strength. And having begun to rebuild our strength, we now seek to engage the Soviet leaders in a constructive dialogue through which we hope to find political solutions to outstanding issues."

However, by late 1983, the dialogue with the Soviets was not going well. The Russians stormed out during talks of arms reduction in Geneva, Switzerland. Fears of a renewed arms race would play center stage during Reagan's campaign for reelection in 1984. His opponent, Walter Mondale, would call for a nuclear freeze while portraying Reagan as reckless in his Cold War strategy with the Soviets.

In the end, buoyed by a resurgent economy and a growing sense of pride felt by the average American, Reagan was granted a second term. Not only that, but Reagan won in a total landslide, as he won forty-nine out of fifty states. He now felt that he had been given a clear mandate from the American people to finish what he had started.

It would be during Reagan's second term that a new Soviet leader by the name of Mikhail Gorbachev would rise to power. Mikhail Gorbachev would prove himself to be just the Cold War partner that President Ronald Reagan needed to dismantle the "Evil Empire" once and for all.

Chapter 10 – Poland, a Polish Pope, and Cold War Solidarity

"We've always had this experience that things take long, but I'm 100% convinced that our principles will in the end prevail. No one knew how the Cold War would end at the time, but it did end. This is within our living experience. I'm surprised at how fainthearted we sometimes are and how quickly we lose courage."

-Angela Merkel

Of all the nations affected by the Cold War, in many ways, Poland seemed to have gotten the shortest end of the stick. In the bygone past, Poland was part of the Russian Empire. After Russia's communist revolution of 1917 and its withdrawal from World War I, the Soviets were forced to give up Poland. By the time of Stalin, the Russians wanted this former piece of real estate back. In fact, they wanted it so badly that Stalin was willing to enter into a deal with the devil himself in order to get it.

Well, Stalin didn't exactly bargain with Satan, but it was close enough—Stalin signed a non-aggression pact with Adolf Hitler. Yes, in 1939, Stalin and Hitler entered into a treaty together. It didn't really declare that the two would be allies, but it did state they would remain neutral in regard to the conquests and aspirations of each other. This meant that if Germany invaded neighboring regions, the Soviets would not intervene, and if the Soviets had military engagements with others, the Germans would not intervene.

Germany launched its invasion of Poland on September 1st, 1939, sending its troops rushing into the western half of the country. The Polish troops were repulsed but holed up in the southeast, where they hoped to hold off the Germans and wait for reinforcements from abroad. Many thought that if they held out long enough that British and French troops would come to their aid. Unknown to the Polish troops holed up in the east, they now had their backs to incoming Soviet troops, which began pouring into eastern Poland on September 17th to make good on the non-aggression pact's agreement that the Soviets would seize the eastern half of Poland for itself.

When the Soviets did show up, there was actually a great deal of confusion on the part of the Poles, who initially thought that the Soviets were part of the international relief force they were hoping would come to their aid. Once the Soviets began their attack, they quickly realized their mistake. Stuck between a rock and a hard place, the Polish troops who survived were forced to retreat right out of Poland and into Romania. In the meantime, France and Britain finally responded and decided to declare war on Germany while steadfastly refusing to declare war on the Soviet Union.

Britain and France knew full well what the Soviets had done, but this inconvenient truth was just too problematic for them to acknowledge. They felt they had to focus all of their efforts against the Germans, who was the closer enemy, and they didn't want to be pulled into a war with the Soviet Union as well. The Soviets, for their part, tried to claim that they were there to protect Ukrainians and Belarussians who lived in eastern Poland since the Polish government was unable to do so. Of course, this was just propaganda, as would later be revealed when the protocols of Hitler's and Stalin's secret plan later came to light.

Through his dastardly dealings, Soviet leader Joseph Stalin had connived a way to extend the Soviet reach into Poland, but it would be short-lived since the Germans would turn on the Russians just a couple of years later. The Germans launched Operation Barbarossa in 1941. By using Poland as a launching pad, they invaded the Soviet Union. After a few years of bloody fighting, the Germans would be pushed back, but throughout the conflict, Poland would become the sight of unimaginable war crimes. After all, it was in Poland that the Germans built and ran the infamous death camp of Auschwitz, along with many other concentration camps.

After the German invasion of the Soviet Union was beat back, the Soviets were able to retake Poland. The Soviets would then refashion Poland into a satellite communist state called the Polish People's Republic. The Soviets would hold on to their communist satellite with an iron grip over the next few decades. However, the Polish people were not going to just sit back and be ruled by Moscow with no say about their own personal affairs. By the late 1960s, protest movements began to emerge.

The protesters were mostly young Poles who found themselves disaffected by a repressive government and a lack of meaningful employment. It's certainly not a coincidence that American protests were at their height in 1968; the Poles were no doubt somewhat inspired by the general feeling of activism that was in the air. These political protests kicked off the 1968 Polish political crisis. In light of these massive protests on college campuses, the Soviet military cracked down on the Polish protesters, seeking to stifle the movement.

But even the Soviet troops couldn't completely subdue the Polish desire for dissent, and it wouldn't be long before it would come bubbling up to the surface once more. In order to head off this dissatisfaction with the communist system, many reforms were issued in the 1970s, but none of them really seemed to gain traction.

Poland would experience another flashpoint of unrest in December of 1970 when the communist government decided to raise the price of several staple food products. This occurred right before Christmas, and it provoked outrage from the populace. Soon, thousands were marching on the Communist Party's HQ in protest. This then led to several more protests and strikes among Polish workers. The Polish communist authorities finally had enough and sent in the troops.

On December 17th, at a shipyard in the Polish city of Gdańsk, things took a particularly brutal turn when security forces opened fire on striking workers. This led to the deaths of forty-two people, with several more were injured. Of course, the Polish people were outraged, and some began to mobilize attempts at insurrection. In the end, though, most knew they stood no chance against the communist troops, and they pulled back to quietly mourn the lives that had been lost.

Periodic strikes would continue to erupt throughout the rest of the 1970s. One bright spot for the Polish during these dark times, especially among those of the Catholic faith, was the ordination of a Polish man as pope. Cardinal Karol Wojtyła was christened Pope John Paul II in 1978. Pope John Paul went on to visit his native Poland in 1979. The crowds that greeted him have been estimated to number some thirteen million people; the reception he received was simply tremendous.

The following year, a reinvigorated Polish people once again led massive strikes against the communist government, and this time around, the government bureaucrats listened. Among the demands that were met was an agreement to scale back government censorship, improve wage earnings, and allow for the development of unions. It was out of these reforms that the Independent Self-

Governing Trade Union, otherwise known as Solidarity, would take shape.

Formed on the grounds of the Lenin Shipyard in Gdańsk, Poland, where so much bloodshed had taken place in the past, the Solidarity union would become a Solidarity movement. It was a movement with not just the best interest of shipyard workers at heart but the Polish people as a whole.

Pope John Paul II was instrumental in galvanizing the Polish people, and you can rest assured that the Kremlin was not appreciative of his efforts. After an attempt was made on his life in May of 1981, some wondered if the Soviet Union may have been behind it. No evidence has since indicated any such connection, but it was certainly of concern.

The screws would tighten in Poland once again, even as Polish citizens felt their situation was improving. In December of 1981, the communist government suddenly declared martial law. On the night of December 12th, security forces began to arrest the leaders of the Solidarity trade union.

The reaction from the United States was rather swift, with measures taken to boycott both the Polish government and the Soviet Union. Sanctions were enacted, and it was made clear to the Polish government that they would not get any relief from the United States until martial law had ended, prisoners were released, and the unions were allowed to function. The recently recovered Pope John Paul would return to Poland in June of 1983 to see if he could help broker a solution to the unrest. He met privately with Poland's communist leader, General Wojciech Jaruzelski, urging him to end martial law and "spare the sufferings" of the Polish people.

Pope John Paul II also held a public audience with about one million Poles, who had gathered for an "outdoor mass." In his speech to those assembled before him, the pope urged the Polish people to continue working toward a "moral victory." The following month, Poland's communist leaders saw the light, and they lifted martial law. From there on out, there was simply no going back for Poland's communist party. There would be no more draconian crackdowns or martial laws declared. By 1989, when the Eastern Bloc began to crumble, the Polish would be at the forefront to assert their freedoms.

In June of 1989, Poland held its first democratic elections since the start of the Cold War. This was then followed by a Solidarity-led coalition government, which was created in August. All of this immediately preceded the "tearing down" of the Berlin Wall, which would occur in November of 1989. It should be noted the Berlin Wall still stood at this point; people were just now allowed to visit their family and friends on the other side of the wall. The wall would begin to be demolished in early summer 1990, and it would be fully destroyed by November 1991.

In many ways, some have theorized that the unique situation of Poland and the Solidarity movement was a major contributor to the cracking of the Iron Curtain. It just goes to show that a motivated populace, a Polish pope, and a little bit of Cold War solidarity can certainly go a long way.

Chapter 11 – Star Wars: The Biggest Bluff in History

"Do not hide behind utopian logic which says that until we have the perfect security environment, nuclear disarmament cannot proceed. This is old-think. This is the mentality of the Cold War era. We must face the realities of the 21st century. The conference on disarmament can be a driving force for building a safer world and a better future."

-Ban Ki-moon

After several decades of old guard communist leaders of the Soviet Union, Mikhail Gorbachev came to power. He was a younger leader of a younger generation, and he soon indicated his willingness for reform. Gorbachev, as it turned out, didn't like nuclear weapons any more than Reagan did. But he needed something to push Reagan toward peace. Something to convince him that nukes weren't necessary.

It was right around this time that Reagan began to talk about SDI (Strategic Defense Initiative) or, as it was often ridiculed, "Star Wars." This was a supposed laser-based system to protect the nation from incoming ICBMs (inter-continental ballistic missiles).

The premise of SDI rested upon the notion that space-based lasers could shoot down any ICBMs headed toward a target as soon as they left Earth's atmosphere. Right before reentry, the orbiting SDI system would fire off lasers to shoot down these missiles. Sounds great, right?

Well, the trouble is SDI didn't actually exist. At least, it didn't exist anywhere other than on some theoretician's white paper. SDI had never actually been developed, yet Reagan spoke of it as if it had already been rolled out. Many explanations for this seeming disconnect with reality have been offered. One is that Reagan, utilizing his skills as an actor, sought to act out the fantasy that SDI was real, and he did it authentically enough to bluff the Soviets into thinking SDI was further along than it really was. This would prove to be a masterstroke on Reagan's part because the Soviets were indeed convinced SDI was all too real. They were terrified at the idea that their nukes might be rendered useless because of this supposed program. However, the more cynical have suggested that this wasn't really an ingenious mind game on Reagan's part but rather the beginnings of his battle with Alzheimer's. This theory contends that Reagan's mental faculties were starting to slip, and he kept confusing proposed future projects as something that already existed.

Either way, all this talk of SDI rattled the Soviets so much that in the arms talks of December 1987, they were willing to sign agreements to reduce armaments. This was the year that Gorbachev also began his policy of "perestroika," allowing a new openness between the East and the West. This meant that, for the first time since the Iron Curtain had descended, a free flow of communication and information was allowed to pass between the Eastern Bloc and the Free World.

This opening of the Soviet public, who had for so long been starved of any contact with the outside world, would lead to even more internal pressure for reform in Soviet society. Gorbachev knew that the Soviet Union was going bankrupt from decades of overspending. The Soviets were spending at least 30 percent of their GDP every year on the military. And now with Reagan touting new high-tech weaponry called SDI, Gorbachev knew that there was no way the Soviets could keep up the pace.

It was for all these reasons that Gorbachev wished to open up an alternative path for the buckling Soviet Union. Gorbachev was indeed a reformer, but he was not a revolutionary. He did not wish to see communism in Russia come to an end; he just wanted to change its direction. Soon enough, the end of communist Russia would be all but inevitable.

In reality, Gorbachev's main aim was to find a way to compete with SDI, and he was shrewd enough to realize that the Soviet Union needed an influx of both cash and innovative research. Gorbachev rightly felt that a more open-minded Soviet society would be needed in order to both improve the economy and get the bright and talented minds of the Soviet Union to brainstorm new ways to meet the challenge of SDI. Gorbachev was essentially looking for another Sputnik moment.

As Gorbachev would later explain his sentiment at the time, "We were increasingly behind the West. Which was achieving a new technological era, a new kind of productivity. And I was ashamed for my country—perhaps the country with the richest resources on Earth, and we couldn't provide toothpaste for our people."

Gorbachev could have easily taken his country down a similar path that communist China ended up taking, in which there was a loosening of the centralized economy and the tightening of the screws of political control. But instead, Gorbachev decided to create a more open society in the hopes that it would be better able to jumpstart both the economy and technological innovation.

However, this newly opened society began to make all kinds of demands that were not always politically expedient for Mikhail Gorbachev. The most palpable of which was the growing cries to tear down the Berlin Wall, which had long stood as the physical embodiment of the Iron Curtain that separated the East from the West. And Reagan, as perfect as ever with his timing, capitalized on this growing clamor in a dramatic way in the summer of 1987. On June 12th, 1987, Reagan stood before the gates of the Berlin Wall and declared to his Soviet counterpart, "General Secretary Gorbachev, if you seek peace, if you seek prosperity for the Soviet Union and Eastern Europe, if you seek liberalization: Come here to this gate! Mr. Gorbachev, open this gate! Mr. Gorbachev, tear down this wall!"

These words would prove to be prophetic. After seeing the futility in having Soviet troops and resources wasted guarding a wall that everyone knew wasn't built to keep people out but rather to keep them in, Gorbachev decided to recall the wall's enforcers back to Moscow in 1989. By doing so, Gorbachev made it known to the world that he was no longer going to keep the Eastern Bloc together by force.

After the Eastern Bloc countries— Poland, Hungary, Romania, Bulgaria, Czechoslovakia, and most certainly East Germany—came to this realization, they began to take advantage of the loosening Soviet grip. All of these nations began to develop policies that gave their societies more freedom. It was around this time that Poland, which was another major focal point of the Cold War, put forth a non-communist government. This would prove to be a major test to Gorbachev's promises of freedom and openness since the Polish people had put this form of government into power through a democratic ballot box.

Many wondered if Soviet troops would begin pouring into Poland to roll back these anti-communist measures, but the troops never arrived. This lack of action in Poland seemed to send a signal to all the other members of the old Eastern Bloc; they now knew they had the green light to take matters into their own hands. And in East Berlin, on November 9th, 1989, this newfound freedom exploded in joyous celebration after the government of East Germany made it known that East Berliners were no longer prohibited from traveling to the West.

The gates of the wall had been opened just as Reagan had requested two years before, and East Berliners began to pour through. Not long afterward, Germans began to tear down the wall itself. It was a seemingly spontaneous yet powerful act, and upon seeing hundreds of young Berliners dismantling the wall that had separated the two countries for so long, neither the local officials in charge nor those from Moscow dared to do anything to stop it.

Germans could be heard happily chanting, "Wir sind ein Volk!" Or, as it translates in English, "We are one people!" And so it was that after a long Cold War of painful separation, Germany had finally been reunited, even as the whole Soviet Union began to rapidly fall apart.

Chapter 12 – The Cold War Comes to a Close

"At the end of the Cold War, the prevailing view in Washington was that the U.S. was strong, and Russia was weak and did not count in a unipolar world. We disregarded Russia's opposition to NATO expansion, the Iraq War, and the U.S. led military intervention in Serbia for the independence of Kosovo."

-Bill Bradley

In the end, the Cold War came to a close without a single shot being fired between the two nations involved. The war was won largely on ideological grounds. People were basically just fed up with the scarcity of communism, both from an economic standpoint and from the standpoint of personal freedom and liberty. But as much as historians will say that communism failed, it's also important to note that capitalism changed during the course of this ideological struggle.

What do I mean by that? Well, when the concept of Marxist communism was first hatched by Karl Marx himself back in the 1800s, capitalism was much different than it is today. Back then, Karl Marx had good reason to criticize the kind of cutthroat capitalism he saw in Europe and around the world. The poor toiled in factories day after day, barely able to make a living and with virtually no hope to rise up the ranks. By the time the Soviet Union ended, it was much easier for a person to prosper under the capitalist system than it was in the days of Karl Marx. For the most part, there were not people dying in the streets in poverty or going to debtors' prisons, as was the case in London in the 19th century.

Of course, there were imperfections and flaws in this system, something which governments are still trying to iron out today. But it still got the job done better than Soviet communism. In fact, the last great supposed communist nation—China—tends to emulate America's capitalist model. Yes, China is still a state-run economy, but relaxations in China's private sector have it geared to be more capitalist friendly.

As much as US President Ronald Reagan hastened the end of the Cold War, he would be out of office by the time it occurred. The two-term president was succeeded by Vice President George H. W. Bush in 1989, so Bush would lead the world through the final days of the Cold War and on to what he termed the "New World Order."

Despite the apparent success of Ronald Reagan's policies, Bush was a Cold War pragmatist, and he knew that even though the Soviet Union was beginning to dismantle itself, the end of the Cold War could prove to be the most dangerous part of the conflict. Bush knew that rushed reforms and revolutions could lead to turmoil and chaos, and when you add nuclear weapons to the mix, it could prove downright disastrous for the whole world. It was for this reason that Bush believed a firm and steady hand needed to be at the wheel in order to make sure that the sinking Soviet behemoth did not wreck all the other ships in the water on its way down.

Meanwhile, Soviet leader Gorbachev was beginning to realize just how unstable the system was. He knew that if it all came crashing down, he himself might be in personal jeopardy. So, he began to look toward Bush for a helping hand out of the sea of discontent that was beginning to pull him under. The Soviet bear was indeed wounded, cornered, and in a dark place. A less scrupulous American leader may have attempted to exploit this vulnerability, but poking the bear could have led to a reaction that the whole world would have regretted.

Bush, however, had a cool, calm head about him, and he knew that he needed to be gentle with the Soviets lest their implosion became an explosion that would injure the United States with its blowback. Along with his experience as vice president, Bush had a long resume of experience in foreign policy from when he was an ambassador to the United Nations and from his time serving as the director of the CIA.

Bush was already an expert on foreign intrigue, and he did not have to be informed by his aides about the ramifications of policy decisions; he intuitively knew what each move on the international chessboard would do. Shortly after the fall of the Berlin Wall, Bush held a pivotal discussion with Gorbachev in Malta, where arms reduction between the two superpowers was once again on the table. These talks would be successful and lead to an additional meeting in July of 1991 in Moscow, which brokered the START 1 treaty.

By the end of the year, the Soviet Union itself would be no more. The complete dissolution of the Soviet Union was actually against Bush's policy at the time. From 1990 forward, Bush was determined to see the end of the Cold War and a drastically scaled-down Soviet Union minus its Eastern Bloc, but he was not seeking a complete dismantling of Soviet power in the region. Without the Soviet Union, Bush rightfully feared that a dangerous power vacuum would ensue.

Therefore, it was for this reason that Bush sought to keep Gorbachev where he was; that way, the US wouldn't have to deal with all of the unknowns of what might happen after Gorbachev was gone. Nevertheless, on August 18th, 1991, Gorbachev was ousted from power—not by those wishing to disband the Soviet Union but rather by those who were wishing to keep it.

A group of hardline communists placed Gorbachev "under house arrest" as they sought to turn the trajectory of the crashing Soviet system around. This group was largely outnumbered by those who wished to see the Soviet regime go, which included much of the Red Army. This lack of support allowed opposition leader Boris Yeltsin—who had already been made president in July of 1991—to step in, stop the coup, and allow the transition to a new government to begin.

In the immediate aftermath of the coup, Gorbachev was able to return to his office. He fully realized that any reform of what was the Soviet Union was too little, too late, and he ultimately decided to let it all go. He tendered his resignation on December 25th, 1991. The following day—the day after Christmas, no less—the stagnation of the old Soviet government came to an end. For many Russians, the end of the old Soviet bureaucracy was the greatest gift they could have been given.

During the last few years of the Soviet Union, times were hard, and even securing the most basic commodities became difficult for the average Soviet citizen. The idea that the nation was a nuclear superpower was of little consolation to the mother who could not get bread to feed her children. These Soviets began to look to Western Europe and the United States, and they realized that there was a better way of life. Why were they suffering like this, yet the free democracies of the Western world prospered?

In many ways, it could be said that the end of the Cold War was brought about by a dissatisfied general population, who looked toward the West and liked what they saw. They enjoyed Western music, Western food, and Western (and Japanese) cars. The Free World was beckoning. Thus, many Soviet citizens adopted a kind of "well if you can't beat em', join em'" attitude when it came to the Western world.

Yet when one considers modern-day Russia and many of its former Soviet satellites, can we really say that they have joined the Western world? The standard of living in Russia for the average citizen is certainly better, but it would be a stretch to say that Russia magically became an Eastern version of Western ideals. In fact, considering Vladimir Putin's Russia, most would vociferously argue the opposite. And it wasn't for lack of trying.

Immediately after the Soviet Union collapsed in December of 1991, a new Russian constitution was adopted, which was heavily influenced by Western thought. In fact, American students from Harvard were on-site to serve as policy wonks and aid with the wording of the document. One can only wonder what Lenin or Stalin might have thought about that! During this process of retooling Russia, the old Soviet one-party system was pushed out in favor of a "parliamentary system," with several parties to choose from. There were so many parties that the average Russian couldn't even keep track of them.

As this new system was being shaped, the Russian press, for a time, also experimented with Western-styled freedoms. This meant that during the years of the first Russian president, Boris Yeltsin, we saw a more "adversarial press" that was not afraid to ask the Russian leader tough questions or even openly criticize policies of the Russian government. However, this experimentation with the freedom of the press proved to be just that—an experiment.

And the experiment did not last much longer than Boris Yeltsin's tenure. Shortly after Vladimir Putin became president, the Russian press was once again restrained. In the 2020s, few in Russia dare to speak out against the Russian government, and those who do may face grave consequences as a result. Russian activist and political opposition leader Alexei Navalny would be a prime example of this.

Navalny had been put behind bars, placed under house arrest, and quite possibly poisoned by the Russian government. It was in the summer of 2020 that Navalny nearly died while on a plane heading from Siberia to Moscow. He ended up in a coma, and after much political wrangling, his allies managed to get him flown out of Russia to Germany so he could seek outside medical treatment.

While he was in Germany, the doctors detected the tell-tale traces of a lethal chemical called "Novichok" in Navalny's system. Was Navalny poisoned simply for daring to stand up to Putin? Vladimir Putin denies having anything to do with the incident, but most believe that he was behind it. And even more alarming, the whole bureaucracy in Russia appeared to do everything it could to aid Putin in his denial.

After all, the Russian doctors who initially treated Navalny were fully capable of detecting signs of Novichok poisoning, yet it took an examination by German doctors for the true cause of Alexei Navalny's sudden illness to finally come out. The idea that Russian corruption is so deeply entrenched that even medical doctors would fake medical reports just in case they might be found unflattering to Putin is alarming, to say the least.

From the dissolution of the Soviet Union in 1991 to Russia in the 2020s, we have seen quite a reversal of fortune as it pertains to Russian governance. It is unlikely that Russia will ever go back to communism, but as it pertains to Western-styled freedoms of democracy, it would seem that such notions have almost entirely been pushed back. Putin and his ilk have made the argument that Western-styled democracy is simply not a fit for Russian society.

Vladimir Putin and his supporters believe that forcing ideas and concepts that are alien to Russian tradition have been disastrous for Russian society in the past. Russia has a long history, and for much of it, the nation has been on a different trajectory than the West. Long before Karl Marx was even born, Russians were sculpting their own unique history, carving out a massive domain that spanned across Eurasia.

Russia is a big country, and the various Russian empires that had been cobbled together in the past were even bigger. At one point, the Russian domain stretched all the way to Poland in the west and to Alaska in the east (the US bought Alaska from Russia in 1867). Throughout Russian history, the only way to control this massive landmass was to have a strongman in charge of an authoritarian, centralized government.

This is the argument that Vladimir Putin has essentially been making ever since he took the reins of power from Boris Yeltsin. Putin contends that Western-styled democracy is just not compatible with Russia. And it seems that even long after the Cold War has come to a close, the world is still trying to come to grips with what it all might mean.

Conclusion: Another Cold War?

Throughout all the decades that the Cold War had been waged, the world had gotten quite used to the idea that we lived in a bipolar framework coalesced by two superpowers. With the collapse of the Soviet Union, America lost its Cold War antagonist and became, for all intents and purposes, the only true superpower remaining. Initially, officials in Washington were tempted to see these developments through rose-colored glasses.

With the fear of nuclear annihilation between two superpowers eliminated, it appeared that a new era was dawning of unheard-of peace and prosperity. In fact, President H. W. Bush coined his own phrase for it, referring to this new epoch as the "New World Order." Bush believed that a new era of world cooperation had dawned. But as is almost always the case, the end of one crisis would bring along another one.

Despite the best-laid schemes of mice and men, one has to realize that the world order has always been in a state of flux. After all, at the end of World War II, the establishment of the United Nations was meant to prevent outbreaks of war, but it was right after WWII came to a close that the Cold War began.

And with the end of the Cold War, it wasn't long before another global conflict emerged, this time in the form of the "War on Terror." During the Cold War, the politics of the United States and the Soviet Union consistently overshadowed most of the developments in the Middle East. Not long after the Cold War was over, Middle East agitators began to emerge on center stage.

Most significantly, the seeds sown during the Soviet invasion of Afghanistan blossomed and bloomed into a global terrorist network called Al-Qaeda, which was led by Osama bin Laden. The attack he launched on September 11th, 2001, took out the World Trade Center and damaged the Pentagon, leaving thousands of Americans dead.

This attack led Americans to refocus their policy as it pertained to the Middle East. With the support of a sympathetic world behind him, at least for the most part, George W. Bush sent American forces into Afghanistan to root out Osama bin Laden's terror network. Thus, the United States decided to try its luck in a place that has been called the "Graveyard of Empires."

Much of the world supported the US invasion of Afghanistan since the 9/11 attacks originated from there, but when Bush decided to widen the War on Terror by sending troops to Iraq, there was a major outcry against it. Bush went to Iraq under the false premise that Saddam Hussein had been stockpiling weapons of mass destruction and supporting terrorists. These claims, which were partially bolstered by a CIA operative named Curveball, proved to be false. This, indeed, became one of the worst curveballs ever thrown to American diplomacy. The United States would spend the next twenty years sorting out the mess that had been made in the Middle East.

While the United States was bogged down in these never-ending wars, China continued to rise in both economic and military power. Even today, United States relations with China grows equally hot and cold.

China has been accused of having unfair trade practices and of consistently violating US intellectual property. China has also been criticized for alleged human rights violations within the nation itself, including claims that ethnic Uighurs are being held against their will in detention facilities in western China (at least as of this writing in 2020). After the election of President Donald Trump, a staunch supporter of tariffs and of taking a hardline against China, a trade war was launched to correct some of China's supposed errors.

Much hope for a peaceful reset between the US and China was fostered by a tentative trade deal that was reached in January of 2020. But the outbreak of the pandemic may have put a stop to that. The idea that this scourge came from China, which possibly concealed and covered up its own initial outbreak of the illness, allowing it to spread, has certainly put a strain on current US/China relations, to say the least.

Some speculate that the US just might be heading into a new Cold War, this time with China as the main protagonist. If this is true, the ramifications would be great. Unlike the United States and the Soviet Union, the US and China are trade partners, and a complete freeze of this trade would have a major impact on both nations. Hopefully, the US and China can learn from the previous Cold War and avoid starting another one.

Part 2: The Space Race

A Captivating Guide to the Cold War Competition Between the United States and Soviet Union to Reach the Moon

Introduction

The Cold War is usually thought of in terms of fear, potential nuclear war, and espionage. While these were elements of the years between the end of World War II and the 1990s, the competition between the US and the USSR had some real benefits. Perhaps the best and most impressive accomplishments during this time resulted from the Space Race.

The Space Race was not something either side set out to win. Initially, the US and USSR were only interested in becoming militarily superior to each other. This competition started by accepting and overlooking the atrocities that the German scientists had enacted on their fellow men during World War II. The best German scientists were given another chance by both nations and many other countries. There is even a joke about this time that depicts the two sides bragging that their German scientists were better than the other's. The next few years revealed just why these scientists were often absorbed into other nations instead of standing trial with other Nazis.

Following the end of World War II, many nations fought to bring the German scientists—especially the German engineers— home to their countries. The scientists had been a major factor in the Germans' long-term success, and, ultimately, the US and the

USSR ensured that the scientists were more evenly divided between the two superpowers. The USSR did not benefit from absorbing German scientists as much as the US because they already had a very adept and knowledgeable primary scientist who had been researching the possibilities of space most of his adult life—Sergei Korolev. The US made more use of their German scientists and the input of others from around the world. While one country worked in secret, the other was far more open. The US's desire to be transparent to help other nations understand what it was doing was the catalyst for the start of the Space Race. Since the USSR could see what the US was doing, it decided to show its superiority through successful firsts in space.

Within two decades of the end of World War II, the two superpowers engaged in a completely different competition. The second half of the 1950s and all the 1960s became a period in which humanity finally did what it had been dreaming of doing for millennia: going into space. When the USSR successfully launched *Sputnik* in 1957, the US realized it was not nearly as far ahead in the Space Race as anticipated. For much of the next decade, the USSR was consistently first in the race to get into space. It successfully sent the first person into space, then the first woman into space, and was the first to orbit the globe. It was even the first to land an artificial device on the moon in 1959. With the pressure on, the US began to focus more on space travel. The USSR had been first to reach the moon (as well as send the first life, including two tortoises, to the moon and back), but the US National Aeronautics and Space Administration (NASA) became the first agency to successfully send humans into the moon's orbit in 1968.

Then, in 1969, the US managed to do what was thought impossible just two decades earlier: it landed a man on the moon and successfully returned him to Earth. Forty years later, no other nations have managed to land a person on the moon.

Following this major success, the Space Race began to die down, and the two superpowers started focusing their attention and efforts elsewhere. Other problems were creating issues that were impossible to ignore back on Earth, and with the major first goals accomplished, it seemed like there wasn't much else to do. The Space Race had all but ended at this point, and it took decades before there was any further significant progress made in space travel. Many at the end of the 1960s could see humans reaching and colonizing Mars within the next fifty years. However, this was not to be the case. It was several decades before anyone even attempted to send orbiters to Mars.

With the crumbling of the USSR and the division of the superpower into several individual nations during the 1990s, the USSR was no longer able to participate in the Space Race. Instead of continuing to push each other through competition, the US and Russia began to work together. Attempts to explore space slowed down but never fully stopped. During the early part of the 21st century, many other nations began to look toward space to see what they could do. By 2020, there was a new Space Race, with several nations trying to achieve what the US and USSR had achieved several decades earlier. This new Space Race has helped revive an interest in space travel on a different level: some private companies have begun to realize their agency to accomplish something that previously was only possible through an entire nation's efforts.

Chapter 1 – The End of World War II, the Fate of German Scientists, and the Future of an Unassuming Ukrainian

Even before World War II began, German scientists had a reputation for their innovation and ability to solve problems. They provided the Germans with a real military advantage through the weapons they devised, including nerve and disease agents. They used psychological warfare to lower the morale of the Allies. When the Allies finally defeated the Nazis and trekked through Germany and the regions the Nazis had occupied, the Allied countries were shocked by the kinds of weapons the scientists had been creating. From a weaponized form of the bubonic plague to other inventions the Allies had not even considered developing, it quickly became apparent to the military leaders that they bringing the inventive German scientists back to their respective countries would give them a distinct advantage. This was particularly true for two emerging superpowers in the post-World War II world: the US and the USSR. The tense friendship that had been maintained during the war ended when it became clear the Nazis had been defeated. Neither side trusted the other, and without an enemy to unify them, the US and USSR began to square off, each promoting its own ideas about what was the best form of governance. In reality, the problem ran much deeper.

At this point, the world was tired of open war. World Wars I and II had left the world unwilling to engage in further combat, especially over something as abstract as ideology. Neither the US nor the USSR wanted to engage in open warfare. Following the end of World War II, both began to look for a different way to wage war that would not cost the lives of soldiers, one in which they could achieve domination through means other than military strength.

The result was a competition to see who could acquire the highest number of former Nazi scientists. In the US, Operation Paperclip was born. This intelligence program brought German scientists into the country, largely in secret. As word spread of the horrors committed by the Nazis in concentration camps, the US government realized the problems that could arise if they were open about bringing German scientists home. The USSR faced a similar problem, especially with the additional level of animosity between the Soviets and Germans. However, both governments decided that bringing such imaginative scientists into their own countries was worth the advantage it would give them in the kinds of weapons they could develop. In total, the US brought eighty-eight Nazi scientists back to the country. It is less certain how many scientists were brought into the USSR, as they were notoriously secretive.

Both countries tried to minimize the activities of their scientists during the time they served under the Nazis. In some instances, the scientists simply did what they were required to do under a ruthless regiment. There were some scientists in the group who had only done what was necessary to ensure they were not killed and their loved ones were left alone. However, it is also true that some of the scientists that both the US and USSR smuggled home were guilty of some real atrocities, whether in the name of self-preservation or indifference. Both nations decided it was more important to have a weapons advantage over each other than to hold these scientists accountable for the atrocities they oversaw.

One of the most notable scientists who was rescued—perhaps without deserving a second chance—was Wernher von Braun. What is interesting about von Braun's time in the US is that, without him, the events of the next few decades would have likely played out very differently. The Nazis had been focused on much more than just weaponry. Back in 1936, they had telecasted the Olympic Games, which were being hosted in Germany. Though not the first broadcast, it was the first to use high frequency signals that likely reached space. While not quite the same as what was to come, this showed that Germany had focused on improving technology overall, not just advancing their weaponry. The US and USSR soon made use of impressive technological advances the Germans had made over the course of the war.

The other notable scientist in the Space Race was Sergei Korolev, a Ukrainian who eventually became another victim of Stalin's paranoia. However, he left his mark on the direction of the space race in the USSR, giving the union a distinct advantage in the race that came to dominate the news around the world during most of the 1960s. Korolev was the man who provided the first real successes of the Space Race.

Wernher von Braun

When it became clear Germany was going to lose the war, its scientists (and many in the military) knew it was only a matter of time before they were captured by Allied troops. There had long been a terrible relationship between the Russians and the Germans, so many German scientists sought to surrender to American,

British, or French soldiers. They feared the way they would likely be treated by the Russians more than the way the nations attacked by Germany would treat them. Wernher von Braun was one of these scientists, and he turned himself over to the Allies in 1945. The Soviets took over the German rocket testing facility in Peenemünde, where von Braun had worked.

Von Braun was the son of a civil servant, born into a noble Prussian family that had supplied many military officers to its country. This meant he had more privileges than the average German or Austrian and likely had a very different understanding of how the government served the people. When he received a telescope for his 13th birthday, he became very interested in space and the possibility of space travel—to the point of neglecting school classes that didn't further his interests. Understandably, this upset his family. Still, he managed to advance more quickly through school because of how easily he learned math and science. He joined the Verein für Raumschiffahrt, a group for people with interest in rocket science. As a part of this society, he gained the attention of the rising German army in 1932. The army offered von Braun a military position to further develop his skills, and he joined. He also started his doctoral program at the University of Berlin. He was hardly aware of the Nazis when they came to power in 1933 because his focus was still almost exclusively on his project: twenty-one-year-old von Braun was often lost in a world of his own.

Von Braun was the technical director of the German project to produce V-2 ballistic missiles, which were constructed by people in concentration camps. Von Braun had been to the facility where the ballistic missile was being made several times as the director of Peenemünde. Both the US government and von Braun himself portrayed his role as a Nazi scientist as apolitical, stating he had done what was necessary to achieve his goal of making it to space. He was called to give an interview for the West German consulate in late 1968 about his time working for the Nazis, and he did give this interview in 1969 during a trial of several Schutzstaffel (SS) personnel. The actual records of his time as a Nazi were released during the 1980s, eight years after he died. It became clear that, far from the political victim he and the US government portrayed, von Braun had been very much aware of where the labor at the facility had come from (even though he had not been involved in the formation of the concentration camp that dedicated workers to the facility). He said that he had been aware of the deplorable conditions and had even negotiated to have some of the personnel transferred so he could help Charles Sadron, a French physicist who had been taken prisoner. While this implicated him in some of the Nazis' crimes against humanity, it was also clear he had been forced to walk a very thin line during his employment for the tyrannical regime. He was arrested by the Gestapo for ten days in 1944 and is often said to have made a Faustian bargain so he could work on a rocket. It seems he was not aware of just how much control the government would have over his project, realizing too late just what he had gotten himself into.

Following his surrender in 1945, von Braun was brought to the US and put to work at Fort Bliss near El Paso, Texas. His war record was covered up so he could continue his work in the US with other German scientists. The team was moved to Huntsville, Alabama, in 1950, where they built missiles. Eventually, von Braun became a big proponent of putting more effort toward space travel. His loyalty to Germany quickly disappeared, as the US made him an American citizen and gave him a prestigious position with control over a project building missiles and rockets.

Though his time with the Nazis has certainly tainted his legacy, there is no doubt that von Braun was instrumental in any success the US had in the Space Race. His interest in space did not diminish over time, and he was even concerned that his record would undermine NASA's reputation. It was partly due to this concern that he waited until after the successful Apollo 7 mission at the end of 1968 before he gave his interview regarding the SS military members.

Sergei Korolev

Unlike von Braun, Sergei Korolev was born to a Ukrainian teacher. Although his father taught Russian literature, Korolev found his interest in aviation. When he was seventeen years old, he designed a glider. When he entered the University of Moscow, this interest shifted to rocket science, which was then in its infancy. After founding the Group for the Study of Reactive Motion, Korolev developed what became the first Soviet rockets in 1931. By 1933, the Soviet military had taken control of the group, which then became the first official part of the development of missiles and other potential weapons. Korolev continued to focus on space while another scientist, Valentin Glushko, worked on propulsions.

After the group had achieved several successes, Stalin's Great Purge began, and Glushko was arrested. Hoping to get his sentence reduced, Glushko joined others in denouncing Korolev, who was then arrested in 1938. Though sentenced to ten years of hard labor, Korolev served less than three years (although he did spend four months in the Gulag). Another political prisoner, Andrei Tupolev, requested Korolev's assistance on projects the military allowed him to work on. Korolev was dedicated to the work, and by the end of 1944, he was put in charge of his own project: trying to make something comparable to the V2 missiles used by the Germans.

With the end of the war in 1945, the Soviets tried to capture German scientists. The US had managed to get many of the top members of the German teams, particularly Wernher von Braun. Still a political prisoner, Korolev was put in charge of a new research center with German scientists. He and his team developed the first intercontinental ballistic missile with a range of 7,000 km, far surpassing the German V2.

Sergei Korolev became known as the Father of the Soviet Union's success in space. However, he did not live to see his biggest success. After being diagnosed with cancer in 1965, he chose to undergo an operation. He died during that operation at the beginning of 1966. Within a month of his death, his project to land a craft on the moon succeeded. Without him, the Soviet space program suffered and began to fall behind the US's. Glushko, who had become Korolev's nemesis after getting him arrested, took over the projects but simply did not have the knowledge or abilities of the man he had once denounced. Even today, the Russians still use the plans Korolev had drawn up for future progress.

Chapter 2 – A Brief Overview of the Cold War Rivalry

Following World War II, there should have been a period of peace and restoration to normalcy. Instead, the world devolved into a tense period known as the Cold War. With most of the world seriously damaged by the war, there were two nations that rose to become rival superpowers: the US and the USSR.

The use of nuclear weapons by the US to end the war brought the world into an entirely new era. Once the USSR acquired that same technology, one of the most dangerous races in world history began: the Nuclear Arms Race. The tension and hostility saw the two nations take the world to the brink of disaster.

When people think of the Cold War, they think of nuclear weapons, the Space Race, spies, and a fight between capitalism and communism. While some of these visions are accurate, others are inaccurate. The fight between the two superpowers took a turn that, while not entirely new, pushed the idea of what was possible.

The End of One War, The Start of Another

Prior to World War II, the very diverse ideologies of the US and USSR inspired dislike between their people and governments, but as both countries pursued isolationist policies, they did not interact much. It was only after World War II that the two countries emerged, wanting to play a larger role on the world's stage.

World War II necessitated uneasy alliances, particularly following the violent overthrow of the Russian monarchy just a few decades earlier. Many of the Allies believed they had struck a bad deal with the rising Soviet Union because the Nazis were the immediate threat. Many of the European nations were devastated after World War II ended, so they were unable to participate in the Space Race. In reality, the USSR didn't have the funds to push for space either, and the Space Race would lead to its bankruptcy since it cost than they had anticipated. Western European nations focused on recovering and restoring thriving economies instead of joining in the push to get into space. The devastation would be their focus for roughly two decades following the end of the war. The fact that they had struck a deal with the USSR created considerable unease, especially as it seemed to recover so much faster from the war than the other nations.

Compared to the other nations who fought in World War II, the US had joined the war late, only entering at the end of 1941 when the Japanese forced its hand. The Soviet Union had also been slow to get involved in the war, having spent several months using the cover of the war to invade neighboring nations. After Stalin's 1935 attempt to form an alliance with other nations (many that later joined the Allies) was rejected, he formed an agreement with Hitler in 1939, making much of the rest of the western world even more anti-Soviet. Only when Hitler sent his military to invade the Soviet Union in 1941 did the two countries became openly hostile, and the Soviets finally joined the Allies.

With the dire situation across Europe and much of Europe under German control, the remaining free European countries did not have much choice. However, Stalin's former alliance with Hitler made it very difficult for the Allies to trust him, and this mistrust did not disappear just because Stalin was finally willing to work with them on their terms. Suspicion and wariness of Stalin continued even after the western nations began to work with the USSR.

The Soviets soon showed why fully trusting them was difficult. While fighting the Nazis, the Soviets continued to expand their area of control under the claim that they were "liberating" nations. Unable to face both the Soviets and the Germans, the Allies could do nothing to stop the hostile overthrow of smaller nations by the Soviets. The resemblances to the way Hitler had worked and what Stalin was doing was not missed by the rest of the Allies, and their mistrust only grew as the war continued. Europe had initially been willing to let Germany take several nations to keep the peace; they did not want to make that same mistake again.

Eastern Europe versus Western Europe

With the end of World War II, the mistrust between capitalist nations and the Soviets intensified. The war-torn nations of Europe were divided between East and West, including Germany, as the USSR insisted on gaining control over some of the countries. Unlike the other European nations, though, the USSR was more interested in growing its power base, not in helping those nations recover. No longer facing a common enemy to unite them with the USSR, Western Europe and the US turned against the aggressive advances of the Soviet Union. Stalin believed that the western European nations would quibble and he would be able to capitalize on this, expanding the USSR into the western parts of Europe. With so many of the western nations devastated from the war, the only other nation that could stand against the USSR was the US. The US provided support to help rebuild European nations, but it also worked to prevent the further spread of communism.

Tensions continued to grow, with Western Bloc nations working to contain communist influences, as stated by the US Congress in 1947. At the time, only the US had nuclear capabilities, and they hoped to use this to keep the Soviets in check. This containment strategy required aiding the western European nations, including Germany. After putting the Marshall Plan in place, the US sought to expand into other economic markets while also providing extensive economic aid. By helping the devastated nations regain control over their economies, the US hoped to ensure that the people in those nations didn't turn to communism to better their lives. It should be noted that what the Soviets called communism was a form of dictatorship, with Stalin clearly at the top. It was not communism as Lenin or Marx had taught it, and Lenin had even warned against letting Stalin get control before he died. Failing to make this distinction, the US worked to expand the system of capitalism when perhaps they should have adopted an approach similar to the strategy that had been used against Hitler. After all, the Soviet Union had grown through hostile invasions, not ideological conversions.

The Trajectory of the Cold War

Once the USSR became a nuclear power, with other nations quickly following suit, war as it had always been fought was no longer possible. Nuclear weapons were simply too deadly, and the launch of any nuclear weapons would likely result in overuse as more nations stockpiled these very destructive weapons. There was a very real possibility that any use of the weapons would trigger an end to humanity as other nations reacted by using their own weapons.

Nations were also starting to realize just how much damage the nuclear weapons caused through fallout. Stockpiling these weapons and making them even more deadly was largely symbolic because most nations understood that using not them would result in dire consequences.

By 1950, the power blocs were in place, and both sides hated each other. While the US was the superpower for the West, European nations were joining in the fight against the USSR through other means. To the east, China was emulating Stalin's approach to communism as it finally ended its civil war and witnessed the rise of Mao Zedong. However, the US and the USSR were the nations with the most power, making them the two representatives of East and West. The idea isn't entirely accurate, as the US was helping to rebuild Japan, which was further east than either the USSR or China, as well as Australia, New Zealand, and other Asian nations with their own forms of government. This later came into play during the battle between the USSR and the US as they began to openly fight proxy wars.

Paranoia grew during this time, with either side believing that the other threatened its very way of life. With traditional war becoming far too dangerous, both sides resorted to other ways of striking at perceived threats. Spies have been around since war was invented, but they were relied upon to act as soldiers during the Cold War. It was easier to deny their existence or to simply trade them in private than to manage actual soldiers on the battlefield.

The Cold War spread well beyond Europe as the rest of the world began to recover following the end of World War II. China had been in political turmoil before the war started, but the factions had put their differences aside to fight the superior powers of the invading Japanese. Once the war was over, the two sides continued their civil war, resulting in the rise of Mao Zedong and Communist China. Like the USSR, China was a dictatorship or oligarchy, not a country that was communist by Marx or Lenin's definition. This was seen by the West as a sign that communism was spreading, fueling their fears.

However, the most interesting and obvious result of the Cold War was the drive to gain dominance in space. By smuggling home German scientists who had been working on rocket technology since before World War II, both the US and the USSR gained significant advantages (though the USSR had a very good scientist of their own they were persecuting at this point). While the other aspects of the Cold War tended to be destructive, the Space Race pushed imagination to the forefront and gave people hope for the future.

Chapter 3 – A Grand Announcement: Both Nations Pledge to Launch Satellites

With both sides firmly established, the world's two superpowers began to try to showcase their abilities to the world to demonstrate which of the two ideologies was superior. Ultimately, their achievements weren't what persuaded nations to adopt one doctrine or the other, but they pushed science well ahead of what many people thought was possible at the time. The US had been the first country to create an atomic bomb, while the Soviet Union was still largely trying to find its footing after its upheaval. The Soviets had a very capable scientist in Sergei Korolev, but with the addition of the German scientists, the USSR quickly caught up to what the US had achieved during World War II. While weapons were important, both sides were focused on something that no nation had chased before the 1950s—the ability to go into space.

The Space Race created a way for the two nations to compete in a way that was far less terrifying and far more engaging than the horrific weaponry they were also developing. Both sides tended to be secretive about the types of weapons they were developing for warfare, but over time, the USSR began to publish more information about its accomplishments.

The positive news of the race to achieve a host of first in space accolades helped ease the tension the two nations had created around the world. Whereas people feared what could happen if there was a nuclear war, the race to be the first to accomplish various milestones in space stimulated the imagination. The Space Race was a positive aspect of the Cold War that is still felt today, as many nations work to go further into space and accomplish new firsts long after it had ended.

Though both nations were working on developing ways to reach space, the Space Race did not begin as a way of encouraging each other. Instead, it was a way of gaining military superiority. However, scientists were often much more interested in the travel aspect, leading the focus to be more on what was possible than how best to use space as a new arena to fight in (and maybe over).

Two Sides Prepare

The beginning of the Space Race wasn't exactly planned. As the two nations eyed each other suspiciously, they were developing missiles, ballistics, and aircraft that would give them an advantage if another war started. The weapons they created were largely deterrents to war because the leaders from both sides understood that the risks of using their most powerful weapons were too high.

The USSR had a head start toward developing ballistic missiles, thanks to Korolev's work. During 1954, he had been instructed to work on an intercontinental ballistic missile, which would have been a first of its kind for the USSR. The missile was named the R-7. While the government was interested in weaponry, Korolev was interested in pursuing his interest in space. After his initial research, Korolev had a coworker and friend named Mikhail Klavdiyevich

Tikhonravov write the *Report on an Artificial Satellite of the Earth* to suggest that the ballistic missile could be used to launch satellites. If he could convince the government that the work could double as a means of establishing a position in space, it would give him a way to keep studying his own passion. To persuade the Russian government to adopt his idea, Korolev included some documents about the US interest in space and their work. Since the US was far more open about what they were doing, it gave Korolev a way to stoke some of the Russian paranoia and persuade the government that it should be considering more than just missiles: it needed to start thinking in terms of what space exploration could do for the USSR.

Though the US hadn't gotten as far as Korolev, it had been steadily working toward getting satellites into space since the early part of the 1950s because people in the US were very interested in space exploration. Ever since the panic inspired by Orson Welles' *War of the Worlds* broadcast over the radio in 1938, interest in aliens and what could be found in space had inspired Americans' imaginations. The US military had been studying the possibility of sending a satellite into space, though it was more of a question of how to do it rather than whether it was possible. The US had released the *Beacon Hill Report* in 1952, a study with fifteen different authors who had worked at the Massachusetts Institute of Technology to do reconnaissance. The report found that satellites that went over the USSR or their territories could be considered a breach of sovereignty. The US had considered conducting its own satellite launches, but this possible violation led to the determination that the satellite launches would need to be approved by a higher authority—namely, the US president.

Just a few years later, another report titled the *Meeting the Threat of Surprise Attack* was released by the Technological Capabilities Panel (a committee formed by the Office of Defense Mobilization). It concurred with the idea that a higher authority was needed to approve launches. To address this, the president's administration wanted to establish a "freedom of space" principle that would allow for the launch of military satellites. By this point, President Dwight D. Eisenhower was listening, and his administration quickly adopted the principle. It had already become a popular discussion topic within scientific circles, so most were prepared for the US government to finally embrace the idea. The same year that Korolev was working to persuade the USSR government to embrace the idea of the dual importance of satellites, the US-sponsored proposal worked to have the International Geophysical Year (IGY) body put out a call for satellite launches that year. The IGY body met in Rome during October of that year (1955).

While the US was simply working to increase recognition and worldwide acceptance of the use of satellites, this prepared the two superpowers for something that neither had anticipated.

The US Announces Its Intentions

Although nearly fifteen years had passed since the attack on Pearl Harbor, in 1955, Americans were still very much aware of the surprise attack and feared a similar attack as the tension of the Cold War worsened. After all, the Soviets had successfully stolen the knowledge of how to build a nuclear weapon and had managed to create their own. This was why the US had established the "Surprise Attack Panel" the Technological Capabilities Panel) responsible for generating the previously mentioned reports. To prevent another surprise attack, the US determined the best way to be aware of would-be attackers was to be able to literally spot the attackers long before they arrived in the US.

To alleviate the concerns of Americans, the US wanted to monitor the USSR territories. To establish this kind of regular surveillance as an acceptable practice, in US President Dwight D. Eisenhower proposed in 1955 that the US and USSR agree to allow flights over each other's territories. His proposal was called "Open Skies." Unsurprisingly, this idea was rejected by the USSR. Stalin had died in March of 1953, leaving the superpower to recover from the loss of a tyrant who often killed those closest to him as he became increasingly paranoid. His successor, Georgy Malenkov, took over the day Stalin died but had only lasted as the USSR leader until September of that same year. Nikita Khrushchev took over the day Malenkov was forced to leave office. Having been in office for less than two years, Khrushchev was moving away from some of the more extreme policies of Stalin's regime. Still, he did not want to appear to agree with the US on topics that might make the USSR seem weak. Rejecting a policy that would allow Americans to fly over its lands seemed like the thing to do.

Following the rejection of this policy, the US government decided it could accomplish longer-term surveillance at a lower cost by sending a satellite into space. The satellite would provide surveillance every time it went over Soviet lands. If the US could do this successfully, it would not be risking any American lives, since the satellite would be unmanned. Secondly, the USSR wouldn't be able to eliminate it since missiles were not powerful enough to reach space. And, even if they could, they were not sophisticated enough to accurately hit a target outside Earth's atmosphere.

Following the IGY body's approval of its satellite project in May of 1955, the US began to move on it. Having adopted a policy of relative openness and honesty about what it was doing, the US made the announcement on July 29, 1955. President Eisenhower spoke to Americans, telling them that the US was dedicated to creating a satellite that would help keep the country safe. He also asked for companies to start submitting proposals to create the satellite.

By making his announcement and calling for proposals, Eisenhower had started the Space Race. Knowing that the US was ardently working on a satellite, the USSR was quick to move forward with Korolev's proposal to use the ballistic missile to help launch a satellite of its own.

The USSR Responds

The US may have been the first to announce its intention to send a satellite into space, but the USSR was already ahead of the idea—its government had just not been as vocal or as focused on it. Korolev's proposal suddenly looked a lot more serious, and they were not about to lose the advantage his keen interest in space gave them. While the US was just starting to look for proposals, the USSR already had Korolev's ideas firmly established. This gave them a nearly two-year advantage.

The talks started internally at first, with Korolev presenting his satellite ideas to the Military-Industrial Commission in August of 1955. The commission soon approved his proposal to use one of its new launchers to send a satellite that weighed 1.5 tons into space. The decision was not unanimous, as there were several missile specialists who thought the focus on satellites would be a problem in the further development of ballistic missiles. Korolev had helped persuade many of the commission to agree by saying he would be able to launch before the start of the 1956 IGY. While there was buy-in for the program, the Soviet Council of Ministers was slow in its announcement, waiting for the early part of 1956 to officially authorize the program.

By the early part of 1956, both the world's superpowers were actively working to send a satellite into space, though the US had no idea just how far behind the USSR they were.

Chapter 4 – The USSR and USA Prepare Their Satellites and Their Sites

With the intentions of the two governments firmly established (whether those intentions were well known to other nations or not), the Space Race began. Now, both the USSR and US had much work ahead to accomplish what they said they wanted to do. The USSR believed they were already ahead with Korolev's work. By comparison, the US was still trying to come up with ideas for launching the satellite.

Both sides needed much more than just ideas and equipment to launch their respective efforts, however. They needed design plans, reliable personnel, and a large amount of space to test their progress. They also wanted to secure the test sites from both spies and the public, as they expected far more failed attempts than successful ones, especially in the early days.

IGY 1957 to 1958

IGY was an international program implemented to collect information and to research and study geophysics and the planetary environment of Earth. It included scientists from eleven major scientific fields, including gravity, ionospheric physics, and solar activity. While there was nothing to specifically aid in satellite development, several of the IGY fields touched on the technology that satellites either used or would benefit from their use.

The IGY was selected to run between 1957 and 1958 because the sunspot cycle would be at its zenith. This period had been established by an international group of geophysicists back in 1950. Its primary purpose was to act as a follow-up to the Second International Polar Year from 1932 to 1933. The initial focus on polar studies quickly widened to encompass eleven fields, as the geophysicists were interested in discussing the many advances in technology, including rocketry. When the International Council of Scientific Unions sanctioned the IGY, seventy nations began to assemble their own scientists to attend, and seventy nations participating in the program.

Both the US and the USSR used this meeting to their advantage. The participants in the IGY not only discussed the results of their studies but also got information from the successful launches of the satellites not long after the end of the IGY. For the two superpowers, it provided a way of learning more about each other's progress. As they worked through their plans, they used some of the information provided during the IGY to try to guess how far along the other country was toward meeting their common goal.

One thing both nations seemed to fail to realize was that their initial timelines were compromised as soon as they declared their intentions, whether publicly or from within their respective organizations, because of the amount of information their scientists did not know. The IGY proved to be a way of understanding more, and the international world eventually benefited from it far more than either of the two superpowers.

The Development of the R-7 and Object-D

Korolev had proposed his satellite to the Military-Industrial Commission back in the summer of 1955 with a timeline that would have resulted in the satellite being launched prior to the start of the IGY. Unfortunately, the delayed authorization put the plans behind schedule by several months. When it was finally approved, the satellite they were to launch was initially named Object-D. It would be developed at OKB-1 (Korolev's design bureau) along with the R-7 missile.

A month after the project was approved, Soviet Premier Nikita Khrushchev visited the site to see the progress being made on the R-7 missile. Realizing that it was a perfect opportunity to push the project along more quickly, Korolev took a mockup of his Object-D to show to the premier. To persuade him of the importance of the project, Korolev showed Khrushchev both the mockup and the plans he had regarding the US satellite. Like the missile specialists, Khrushchev was concerned that the satellite would adversely affect the missile program's progress. Korolev persuaded the premier of the project's value and that it would not interfere with the missile project. With this assurance, Khrushchev endorsed what soon became the most advanced space program of the time. It was Korolev's persistence that ultimately pushed the USSR to be the leader in the Space Race.

One of the reasons Korolev was successful in getting the premier's endorsement was that he showed that the R-7 intercontinental ballistic missile was already well along in the development process. Since they were planning to use the R-7 to launch their satellite, they were much further along than the US, which was opting to create an entirely different rocket for its efforts to get a satellite into space. Planning to use a model that was already in development enabled the USSR to work on both ballistic missiles and satellites at the same time.

Selecting a Proposal and Choosing a Site

Three primary proposals were considered by the US:

1. The US Air Force submitted what they called the "World Series plan." This plan included a satellite that weighed as much as 5,000 pounds, launched by an Atlas missile.

2. The Army submitted Project Orbiter, which included a satellite that was only five pounds and would be launched with a Redstone missile.

3. The Naval Research Laboratory submitted the Project Vanguard proposal, which had more capabilities than the Project Orbiter. Unlike the other two proposals, the Vanguard required the development of a new rocket to get it into the atmosphere; the new rocket would be based on the existing Viking sounding rocket.

The team reviewing the proposals quickly ruled out the US Air Force's proposal because they thought it posed a potential problem to missile development. It was harder for them to eliminate the Army's proposal because it was both further along (since they would not need to create a new rocket) and more cost-effective. However, the Vanguard offered a more in terms of scientific capability thanks to the wide range of instruments it included. This was far more aligned with the goals of the IGY. For a short period, the committee considered merging the two proposals, using the Vanguard satellite with the rocket proposed by the Army. Ultimately, the rivalry between the two branches of the US military led the committee to decide not to mix proposals. The two proposals were put to the vote, and the Vanguard was selected by a single vote. In August 1955, the US selected Project Vanguard to serve as a science satellite for the IGY.

On September 9, 1955, the US officially started the project, building six vehicles with the hope that one of them would be successful. With a budget of $20 million and eighteen months to complete the six vehicles, the US finally began to plan for its satellite launch.

Today, this decision is criticized because it put the US behind the USSR, though there was no way for the US to know that at the time. Had they gone with either of the other two proposals, the US would have been largely on equal footing with the USSR. One other important consideration at the time was to have the satellite appear to be a joint effort between the government and the private sector. The Vanguard met this criterion and helped create the image that the US was working toward an Open Skies precedent. The goal was to establish that private companies could have satellites flying over other nations without being considered a threat. If people associated satellites with governments, it would make the satellites seem more sinister and perhaps be less acceptable.

The US was working toward this goal when the USSR announced it would launch a satellite during the IGY. With many Americans seeing this as a potential threat, they quickly looked to the US government to ensure they were first. Unfortunately, the selection of the Vanguard almost guaranteed the US would be second, with far more to develop and test than the USSR did. It also had no use as a military tool since it did not rely on a ballistic missile to lift a heavy payload.

With both sides finally committed to their programs, it was just a matter of time before one of them was successful. They both had the necessary scientists, sites, and tools. Their approaches were significantly different, largely because they had very different assessments of each other. While the USSR was constantly monitoring the US for its progress, the US continued to assume its own superiority. The US had been the first to develop working nuclear weapons and had more advanced weapons, so it believed it would be the first nation to reach space. The USSR had made an announcement, but it was far more difficult to know its progress, considering it did not broadcast details, and its program was tightly locked behind military security. By comparison, the US government had plans that were more accessible, particularly as it was working with the private sector. This did not mean the Soviets were always accurate in their assessment of how far the US had progressed, but the Soviets did tend to overestimate the Americans, pushing them to act faster and to work longer hours to stay ahead. This eventually paid off in 1957.

Chapter 5 – Russian Accomplishes Several Firsts with Sputnik 1, 2, and 3

As the US felt comfortable it would be the first to successfully launch a satellite, Korolev became increasingly concerned the nation's confidence would be justified. To be the first to succeed, he faced the Presidium of the Soviet Academy of Sciences to request additional funds during September of 1956. He and his team were already behind schedule, and he saw the dream of being first slipping away. This fear was largely based on a report (which turned out to be incorrect) that said the US had tested a launch in Cape Canaveral earlier in the month. Though the report seems to have indicated the launch failed, the truth was that the US had not advanced that far quite yet.

Korolev's concerns were further compounded by issues the team was having with the R-7 engine. They had modified it so that it could launch a heavy satellite, but the engine's thrust levels were insufficient. Fearful of losing their advantage, Korolev began to drive his team to work longer hours to resolve the issues, but it became clear they needed to change their plans since they were too far behind schedule to meet their target launch date. Knowing they couldn't possibly succeed, Korolev finally adjusted the plan.

At the beginning of 1957, the team reduced the weight of the satellite to reduce the amount of power and thrust needed to get the satellite into the atmosphere. Still believing in the report that said the US was already testing rockets, Korolev got approval for the changes. At the time, he was concerned the US would be successful within the next few months, a fear that was unfounded.

New Satellites

Not sure how much time he had before the US would be successful, Korolev tried to come up with a solution that would work better with their current progress. This resulted in two simpler satellites called the PS-1 and PS-2, which were only about 220 pounds each. PS was short for *prosteishy sputnik*, which translates "simplest satellite," indicating that they were switching to a simpler version to ensure they beat the US into space. This change required approval to proceed, which was finally given by the Soviet Council of Ministers in the middle of February 1957.

When the IGY started at the beginning of July 1957, the Soviets were testing their work. The US Central Intelligence Agency (CIA) had learned of their progress and was trying to warn the Eisenhower administration without rousing too much concern. Korolev likely did not know that the US was far behind his work, which worked in his favor because it helped to drive him to try to finish the work before the US. His drive ensured that the USSR would be first in getting an artificial satellite into space. He and his team suffered three failures by the end of July, and not until August did they finally have a successful test of the R-7.

Once it had a successful test, the Soviet Union decided to announce its progress to the world. This announcement was met with skepticism in the US, and the USSR continued to make progress without the US feeling driven to beat them. When the USSR successfully launched the R-7 a second time in the early part of September, it didn't celebrate with nearly as much fanfare: it had already been the first nation to successfully test an intercontinental ballistic missile. Whatever the reaction from the US, there was no need to make a stir again. The Soviet Union was more interested in being successful at the next stage—getting a satellite into space.

The USSR had initially targeted September 17 as the date to accomplish this, but with several failures over the summer and the second successful launch on September 7, the target date was adjusted so they could ensure any issues were worked out prior to launching a satellite. A new date was approved: October 6, 1957. Paranoid that the US was making advances faster than it was admitting, or perhaps in response to the USSR's successes, Korolev had the date moved to October 4. They had to make further modifications to the R-7 with the lighter satellites.

Having created two smaller, modified satellites, Korolev's team planned to use PS-1 for the October 4 launch. With everything apparently ready, the USSR prepared to become the first nation to send an artificial object into Earth's atmosphere.

Sputnik 1

The PS-1 was silver and round with four antennas that extended from the core of the satellite. It was roughly twenty-two inches around and looked fairly innocuous. The core of the satellite was about the size of a basketball, but with the four antennae, it ended up being bigger than a person. The outside was made from an aluminum alloy. The most threatening-looking part of it was the radio beacon that flashed as it pinpointed different places on the planet's surface.

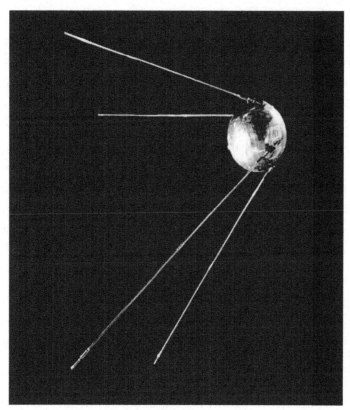

Sputnik 1
(https://live.staticflickr.com/8041/8052668653_4c784d13f6_z.jpg)

Since Sputnik was not the original satellite, its abilities and lifespan were greatly reduced. It was considered an elementary satellite. With its reduced capacity, its primary purpose was to simply add radio transmitters into Earth's orbit. The USSR had already learned about the need to protect against heat, so the outside included a heat shield sphere. The next layer of the satellite was a pressurized sphere to protect the silver-zinc batteries and radio transmitters inside, which created a beeping noise.

On October 3, Korolev and his team began to prepare for the launch. The modified R-7 was moved onto what they planned to use as the launchpad for the first and future launches. The R-7 spaceport has come to be known as the Baikonur Cosmodrome, and it was developed by Korolev's friend Tikhonravov. The R-7 rocket that was originally planned had been changed so much that it was given a new designation, 8K71PS. Much of what was included on the R-7 was removed for the model to launch the PS-1, including the military warhead, hardware designed to measure launch data, a considerable amount of avionics to monitor vibration, and the radio control system.. Since they had switched to a less robust satellite, much of the planned tracking system originally established for Object D was not in place for the launch of the PS-1. Only the necessary systems were ready by the launch. In February 1957, they had established the radio transmitter specifications, and those were verified before the launch.

Once the equipment was set up, the Russian team began to fuel the rocket at 5:45 a.m. Sixteen hours passed before everything was ready and the R-7 launched the PS-1 into space. Six minutes after the rocket launched, it ejected the PS-1 into the atmosphere. At some point, the satellite received a new name, Sputnik, which roughly translates to "traveling companion" or "fellow traveler" depending on the translator. It would come to be known as *Sputnik 1*. Today, the term *sputnik* is often synonymous with the term satellite, showing just how important this remarkable accomplishment was.

At night, the satellite could be seen orbiting the Earth. It took less than one hundred minutes for Sputnik to fully travel around the world. Even on cloudy nights, it could sometimes be seen as it passed overhead, the beeping from the radio transmitters helping observers pinpoint its location. During its time in orbit, it had five specific objectives:

- Test the method of launching a satellite into orbit

- Calculate the lifetime of the satellite in orbit to determine the atmosphere's density

- Try both the radio and optical functions placed in the satellite

- Test radio wave propagation for satellites in the Earth's atmosphere

- Check the pressurization principles on the satellite

As soon as the satellite began to orbit the Earth, Soviet news began to broadcast information about the successful launch. This could have been premature since the satellite had not yet fully orbited. Still, even if it had not fully orbited the Earth, it was the first artificial object in space. Flight controllers detected the Tral telemetry system operating in the satellite as *Sputnik 1* made its second revolution. Both the satellite and the rocket booster reached lower-Earth orbit.

Korolev's role in this accomplishment is undeniable, as he was the one who kept pushing for the USSR to strive for space instead of focusing solely on developing weapons. However, his friend Tikhonravov was responsible for much of the project's successes. Having been a member of GIRD, one of the early Soviet rocket research organizations, Tikhonravov had extensive knowledge about missiles and participated in numerous studies into what was necessary to orbit the planet. Both these figures receive most of the credit for what was accomplished with Sputnik, and they continued to play key roles over the course of the Space Race. Several other notable figures included Mstislav Vsevolodovich Keldysh and Dmitry Fedorovich Ustinov. Keldysh, a scientist who was a strong proponent of developing calculations and mathematical solutions to space flight, was instrumental to the success of Sputnik. Ustinov, who came from a working-class family, became the Deputy Chairman of the Soviet of Ministers, and his dedication and political support helped ensure *Sputnik* had the resources necessary to succeed. Without these two figures, Tikhonravov and Korolev alone may not have ensured that the USSR achieved the distinction of the first nation to reach space.

The batteries at the core of *Sputnik 1* were not made to last, and after just twenty-two days, they died. *Sputnik 1* continued to circle the Earth for a few more months (staying in orbit for roughly three months) before falling back to Earth. It had only reached the lower part of Earth's orbit, so it was not going to remain in orbit for long. On January 4, 1958, Sputnik finally began to fall back to Earth, burning up as it re-entered the atmosphere.

Sputnik 2

Following the rousing success of *Sputnik 1* and the lack of response from the US (at least in terms of establishing its own success), the Soviet Union continued to press to achieve other firsts. While *Sputnik 1* was no longer sending signals, it was still orbiting the Earth when *Sputnik 2* was prepared. This time, the USSR was determined to send a living creature into space. On November 3, 1957, the Soviets prepared *Sputnik 2*, which weighed more than 1,100 pounds so that it could protect the living creature—a dog named Laika. The date was selected by Khrushchev, who wanted to mark the 40th anniversary of the Bolshevik Revolution that had removed the Russian monarch and ushered in Communism.

The history of animals in space pre-dates the Space Race. Fruit flies were the first living organisms to reach space and then return when the US launched them on a V-2 rocket in 1947. In 1950, a mouse was shot into space and died. This initial failure was followed by a few successful attempts where the rockets that housed the animals were robust enough that the protection didn't disintegrate. Since the exterior was strong enough to handle reentry, the parachutes were fully functional when they needed to deploy. The first monkey, named Albert II, was launched into space in 1949 and safely returned with the use of a parachute. His predecessor and two successors all died when the rockets carrying them failed.

The reason Laika's launch received so much attention was that she would not be immediately returning to Earth. Laika was a stray mutt (a mix between a spitz and a husky) taken off the streets of Moscow to become the first living creature to go to space. She was chosen from a group of other stray female dogs after passing a series of tests that sought the most docile and obedient dog from the group. The potential dogs were tested to see how they would react to loud noises and changes in air pressure, as the dog would experience these during the initial launch. A little dog named Kudryavka, or Little Curly, was selected because of her placid nature and how well she reacted to the changes. A back-up dog named Albina was chosen, as well. The public saw Kudryavka as the Soviet news introduced her to the people. She barked a lot during her time on air, gaining her the name Laika, or "barker." Both Laika and Albina had small medical devices implanted into their bodies so that their heart rate, blood pressure, breathing pattern, and movements could be monitored.

When it was time to start preparing for the launch, Laika was put into her own little specially-designed spacesuit, which was meant to keep any waste from damaging the instruments onboard. The launch occurred at 5:30 a.m. on November 3, 1957, and it had a G-force that measured five times higher than the usual pull of gravity. The Soviets monitored Laika, and her vital signs showed that she was frightened by the launch, with her heart rate tripling.

They did not plan for the dog's safe re-entry, though. Given only one meal and enough oxygen to last for seven days, the unfortunate Laika died while orbiting the planet. They could not offer more meals to the dog because it would have put the satellite over the payload the rocket could manage. One physician was said to have felt bad, and despite the protocols, she gave Laika a meal prior to lift off to help the dog survive as long as possible.

Though they knew that Laika would not survive, they had thought she would survive for at least seven days. Had she lived long enough for the oxygen to be used up, it was thought she would die a painless death about fifteen seconds later. However, it wasn't the loss of oxygen that killed her. The USSR did not realize what kind of temperatures she would encounter once she was in orbit. Her vital signs showed that she did reach orbit, but she did not survive long after that. About 103 minutes after launch, Laika entered orbit. She had a rapid increase in temperature, which meant she had lost her heat shield. By the time the capsule was making its fourth revolution, the temperature inside was more than ninety degrees, and they don't think she was alive much longer than that as the temperature continued to rise.

Sputnik 2 was in orbit for a few months longer than the first satellite. It is said the Soviet Union falsified the documents to make it sound like Laika survived for days after the launch instead of the few hours she likely experienced. An initial belief was that she could be brought back safely, but the Soviets admitted she died after *Sputnik 2* had been in orbit for nine days.

This event became one of the first major points of contention in the Space Race. Though animal rights weren't nearly as well established as they are today, there was an outcry from many nations about the Soviet's plan to send a dog into space without any intention of returning the dog safely back to Earth. Her fate has received a lot more attention in recent history, and the dog has received attention in different forms of media.

What the world learned about space during Laika's short time in space was that life could be sustained with proper planning and care. The biggest obstacle to the trip was the return, which generated unimaginable heat that destroyed the early Soviet satellites. Ironically, she was not the first dog to reach space, though. The Soviets had adjusted German V-2 rockets following the end of World War II that sent dogs into space, then parachuted them back to the planet. However, Laika was the first to spend more than a few fleeting moments in space as she orbited Earth.

Sputnik 3

Following two successful launches that firmly established the USSR as the dominant nation in space travel, the push to do more was temporarily alleviated. With his schedule largely all his own, Korolev returned to focusing on Object-D. Following the events of the last two launches, he decided to make two of them.

The originally planned satellite, Object-D, was finally completed by the beginning of 1958. By this time, the US had finally reached space, but the USSR was still well ahead, having sent a living creature to space (though they failed to sustain life). With those two successes, Object-D was finally prepared for launch, and it was named *Sputnik 3*. This satellite was more specific and ambitious than the stripped-down satellites launched as *Sputnik 1* and *Sputnik 2*.

In April of 1958, the USSR began preparing to launch Object-D into space. On April 27, they completed the launch of the much heavier satellite. For the first time, one of their planned launches did not go as planned, and the rocket with the Object-D failed to reach orbit. Less than two minutes after launch, the team watched the rocket disintegrate and crash back to the ground. The team went to check the crash site and were surprised to find that the satellite had not been destroyed by the fire and subsequent crash. As they returned with it to the facility, it began to short circuit, starting a fire that nearly destroyed the satellite. Given the number of problems with the first one, Korolev decided to use the backup satellite.

A new launch date was set for May 15, 1958, and this time, the launch was virtually flawless. By this time, the US had launched more satellites into space than the USSR, but the satellites were not as advanced as *Sputnik 3*.

Sputnik 3 had a recorder that failed to work properly, which meant it was not able to complete all the planned objectives. At nearly 3,000 pounds, it was the heaviest satellite to reach space. While the recorder did not work as intended, the twelve instruments on board provided data on a range of Earth measurements, including the upper atmosphere, radiation, cosmic dust, and the Earth's magnetic fields. The other instruments worked, though the data was not able to be recorded.

In April of 1960, *Sputnik 3* finally returned to Earth.

Chapter 6 – Americans Play Catchup

The reports that had lit a fire under Korolev and driven him to expedite his plans so late in the game were gravely mistaken. Just as he and his team were finding significant problems with their work, the US was experiencing its own problems as it worked to build both a satellite and a new rocket to get the satellite into space. Also like Korolev, the US team had to request more money to make changes and adjustments based on what they found when they tried to put their ideas into practice.

As the cost of the Vanguard development and testing increased, the program faced the threat of reduction (though it wasn't at much risk of cancellation). Only when the US was forced to realize it was not leading the world did it feel a similar motivation to catch up to the Soviet's success.

A Problem of Budget

The original of $20 million ballooned into a $110 million effort, and people within the scientific community began to question if the program was worth the price tag. After all, the US still believed it would be the first to launch a satellite into space, and there were no reliable reports to indicate it had any reason to be concerned about the USSR's progress. A memorandum about the unexpected costs was sent to the president to address the issue.

Despite the budget issue, the US was finding successes in its testing by May 1957. The team pointed to these successes as proof that the ballooning costs were worth the effort because they had gone from the planning stages in the fall of 1955 to testing by the spring of 1957. John Hagan, Vanguard's program director, also pointed out that the success of the program would offer a wealth of scientific benefits, the declared reason the US was dedicating so many resources to the effort. To play on Eisenhower's idea of what was possible for the future, the director pointed to the way the achievement would greatly benefit the scientific community and change the direction of the world as people realized that space was achievable. Unfortunately for Hagen, Eisenhower was far more interested in the project's costs and did not let them continue to balloon regardless of the possible benefits. The president accused the team of creating satellites that he had not approved. He also said that the prestige would come from the success of the launch, not the instruments that would provide scientific readings. The primary reason Eisenhower was willing to let the program continue was that the US had announced it would launch a satellite. Americans were excited and expectant, and the global community and the IGY had been told that the US would go through with it. This led Eisenhower to believe it was necessary to put money into the program, but he was beginning to think it wasn't the progressive program he once thought it was.

Since he had little interest in seeing the progress of the program that was becoming increasingly expensive, he didn't think it was necessary to complete all six of the satellites since the program would achieve its goal as soon as one of them was successfully launched. He felt no urgency because the US was still confident that no one else was anywhere close to achieving its goals. However, they were well behind the USSR by this point, as Korolev and his team were preparing to test (if not already testing).

During the early part of July 1957, the CIA reported that the USSR was making progress much faster than the US had expected. Based on what it had learned, it seemed possible the Soviets would successfully launch a satellite by the middle of September, around the anniversary of Russian rocket pioneer Konstantin Tsiolkovsky's birthday. The CIA informed both the Deputy Secretary of Defense and Eisenhower's administration. The news was largely brushed off with the idea that it could be a false report to get them to spend more money.

That all changed on October 4, 1957, with the announcement that the USSR had more than successfully tested a satellite. *Sputnik 1* was more than just a known threat—it could be seen tearing across the skies in the US on a clear night. The paranoia that came with this sight caused the US to ramp up its efforts as the Americans found themselves slipping from an assumed comfortable lead to a distant second to the USSR. This was a concern not only because of the implications that the USSR could monitor the US but also because it showed that US military and science superiority was not as secure as most people thought.

With *Sputnik 1* traveling over the US about seven times a day, the American people wanted to know what the US government was doing to protect them. This question was slightly louder than the demands to know how the USSR managed to beat the US into space.

Soothing the Concern

The first problem with the Soviet's success was not an indication of a technological failing; it was the reaction of the American people. After all its modifications, *Sputnik 1* was about 185 pounds, which was far heavier than the Vanguard that the US was developing. As impressive as the vision of *Sputnik 1* was, it inspired a sense of dread. The US was not the first nation to reach space, and there was also fear that the USSR would initiate a surprise attack. The events since the tragic day at Pearl Harbor less than two decades earlier were still very fresh on the minds of the American people. While there was no physical war being fought, Americans questioned just what was happening with the project that had been announced back in 1955. The US had been the first to announce its intentions, yet the Soviets had managed to beat them into space. If the Soviets could launch a heavy satellite into space, they had the necessary technology to launch a ballistic missile at the US. Since the USSR had successfully tested their own nuclear bombs, the threat was even greater.

Having devalued the project and ignored the indications that the Soviets were nearing success, Eisenhower and his administration were forced to face their own failings and lack of vision. The unexpected success by the Soviets, something that they had been warned about months before it happened, was a wakeup call that made the US start to take the Vanguard project far more seriously.

As *Sputnik 1* passed over the US, unnerving Americans, Eisenhower tried to downplay what it meant. Having already expressed his displeasure at the cost of the Vanguard project, he was soon forced to realize the mistake he and his administration had made. Instead of leading the world into space, the US was playing catchup to the USSR.

The US suddenly had a reason to make space exploration their top priority, and soon, money was flowing into the Vanguard program.

A New Drive to Succeed

Although Eisenhower insisted there was nothing to fear, reports on the progress of the Vanguard began broadcasting to the American people. US scientists were working on not only the Vanguard rocket but also a satellite called the *Explorer 1* that would be launched into space. Live reports were given to help to show the people that the US was not far behind the Soviets. Unfortunately, the reporters ended up broadcasting just how far behind the US was when they inadvertently broadcasted the explosion of the Vanguard to American homes.

It was a horrible setback. As the news came up with clever headlines like "Kaputnik," the officials decided that they would need to change their approach. As they discussed what to do, they decided to switch to the Juno rocket. They also decided to work in secret, more like the USSR had done, to ensure there weren't any more public embarrassments that would reduce the people's trust in what the US could accomplish. They had managed to retrieve the satellite, but it was damaged because of the explosion of the rocket.

Now working in secret at Cape Canaveral, the team moved forward with the launch. When they felt that they were nearly ready, they let the media know that they were preparing to try again. Fully aware that the USSR had managed to launch two satellites into space, including the ill-fated journey of Laika, the US prepared for its second attempt to launch a satellite into space. The team was ready on January 31, 1958, but instead of using the Vanguard again, it used the rocket that the US Army had suggested, one that had been worked on by von Braun and his team. The new rocket was called the Jupiter-C. At the same time, Jet Propulsion Laboratory had been designing and building the satellite, which they completed within three months.

The US successfully launched its first satellite into space on January 31, 1958. Since the primary purpose for the satellite wasn't military use, the satellite worked to learn more about space. *Explorer 1* was more than just a satellite; it was a cosmic ray detector. As it orbited, it measured the radiation around Earth. Scientists were surprised to find that the count was lower than they had expected. The measurements and results were run by Dr. James Van Allen. Based on findings, he began to theorize there was a belt of radiation around the Earth, a theory that was confirmed by the second US satellite. The US may not have been the first to reach space, but it was the first to transmit signals back from space. *Explorer 1* also provided scientific data that helped scientists better understand the area around the Earth's atmosphere. Repeated trips into space found that the radiation belt trapped radiation, and the belts were called the Van Allen Radiation Belts in honor of the project leader. Both the USSR and US would have to take this finding into account later as they sought to send people further away from Earth. At this time, the US was behind the USSR in what they had accomplished, but they were collecting data that would give them a distinct advantage later. While the USSR focused on accomplishing as much as possible as quickly as possible, the US was trying to learn from each mission. The US met many of the same goals a bit behind their Soviet counterparts because they were also gathering data. They also had an advantage because they were working with other nations who were interested in space travel but were still recovering from the devastation of World War II. This desire to collaborate would further slow the US in the beginning, but it would significantly boost its abilities to accomplish feats at a steady pace.

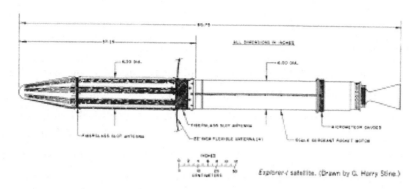

Explorer 1 (https://upload.wikimedia.org/wikipedia/commons/f/f0/ Explorer1_sketch.jpg)

While slower to reach space, the US sent *Explorer 1* higher than the *Sputnik*s had gone. Since *Explorer I* was higher, it orbited the Earth every 115 minutes, with fewer than thirteen orbits each day. It began to transmit information back to Earth on May 23, 1958, and fell back to Earth more than twelve years later on March 31, 1970, having lasted far longer than any of the first *Sputnik*s. It was able to remain in space longer because it had gone so much higher over the planet.

A launch of *Explorer 2* was attempted on March 5, 1958, but it failed. Unlike the first failed launch attempt, this time the problem was that the Jupiter-C rocket's phases did not function as expected. The US's next attempt to send *Explorer 3* into space was successful on March 26, 1958. It continued to function until June 16, 1958.

Between the failed launch of *Explorer 2* and the successful launch of *Explorer 3*, the US mirrored the progress of the USSR. After abandoning its original satellite in favor of something more certain, the US returned to its original satellite for the third launch. On March 17, less than two weeks after the failed attempt to launch *Explorer 2*, the US successfully sent *Vanguard 1* into space. Well ahead of its time, *Vanguard 1* was solar-powered. This satellite could better study the shape of the Earth and reported back that it was asymmetrical, more closely resembling a pear than a ball. This satellite also has the distinction of being the oldest satellite in space, as it is still orbiting the Earth as of 2020. However, it stopped transmitting back in 1964.

By this point, the US had sent one more satellite into space than the USSR and had obtained data from its satellites. However, the US had not managed to create anything that could support life to reach space. This gave each side different advantages, although the US was far more open (while not necessarily more honest) about what it achieved. After its very public early failures, the US was no more eager to discuss its failures than the USSR was. Still, there were a few televised failures since the US continued to broadcast many of the launches.

The US successfully launched *Explorer 4* on July 26, 1958, a few months after *Sputnik 3*. Then the launch of *Explorer 5* failed, showing that both the US and USSR were still trying to find their footing. There remained as many failures as successes since little was known about space when the Space Race began. The failures also showed that both needed to move more carefully as they sought to be the first to reach the ultimate goal of sustaining life in space and returning that life safely.

The Formation of the National Aeronautics and Space Administration

With the launch of *Sputnik 3*, the US decided that its approach to coordinating and managing space exploration simply wasn't working—it was again falling behind. A Congressional hearing was held to create an agency with the sole purpose of running the American space program. Like the efforts up to that point, the dedicated agency would be a civilian agency, not a military one (something that is still true today). The creation of the National Aeronautics and Space Administration (NASA) was approved by Congress through the *National Aeronautics and Space Act* in July

1958. Eisenhower signed the act into law roughly a month later, and NASA officially began to operate at the beginning of October 1958. By the time the high-tech *Sputnik 3* fell out of orbit in 1960, NASA was helping to close the gap between the two superpowers.

NASA was intended to prove that the US was not just developing ballistic weaponry; it was serious about scientific findings. Therefore, a second agency attached to the military was started to keep ballistic weaponry separate from space development. Called the Advanced Research Projects Agency, it also began operating in 1958.

Chapter 7 – Different Approaches to Getting the First Men in Space

The IGY was as exciting and busy as the two superpowers had promised. Between 1957 and 1958, they had both made significant strides toward space exploration. However, the technology used to launch the satellites into space was based on weaponry. The US and USSR achieved their rockets so quickly because they used the knowledge of German scientists, who had been close to completing ballistic missiles when World War II ended. Using this technology enabled the two superpowers to significantly reduce the time it took to start launching rockets and satellites.

As the USSR had found, rocket-launching technology was not ideal when dealing with living creatures. The ultimate goal was to achieve space travel, and getting a person into space was only the first challenge of many. They had expected Laika to last much longer than she did, but they had not known about the heat in Earth's atmosphere. Later, the two nations would learn that, away from Earth, temperatures were deadly cold. There was a lot to learn, but the final question was how to get people safely back from space. After the backlash from intentionally launching a dog into space knowing that she would not survive, neither nation was willing to risk sending people into space without a plan to bring them back safely. Figuring out how to achieve this would take them a while longer, and they continued launching different satellites to conduct tests.

The Studies, Failures, and Accomplishments of the Soviet Union

Between 1957 and 1961, both the US and USSR divided their time and resources between developing a way of launching a person into space and safely returning them and continued work on satellites. The US was dedicated to making satellites as scientifically beneficial as possible, while the USSR was more focused on travel.

After their two successful launches in 1957, the USSR only launched one satellite in 1958. *Sputnik 3* was a significant success, but it was not their only attempt to launch more satellites into space. During 1958, the Soviets had only attempted to send two satellites into space—the initial failed launch of *Sputnik 3* and then its success. Following *Sputnik 3*'s successful launch on May 15, the USSR did not attempt another launch until January 1959. They attempted to send *Luna 1* on January 2, which was a partial success. It was the first artificial craft to make it to the moon, marking the beginning of a series of crafts that the USSR would launch toward the moon. *Luna 1* would reach the moon, but instead of landing on the moon, the satellite shot past it. Since it did not have any propulsion system of its own, this could not be corrected. As it moved away from Earth, the orange glow of the trail left by the craft could be seen back on Earth. *Luna 1* was not only the first satellite to go close to the moon but also the first craft to have left Earth's orbit. It was pulled into orbit around the sun after losing contact with the USSR about sixty-two hours after it was launched. Today, *Luna 1* is circling the sun, taking about 450 days to complete a full orbit. However, it is small, making it nearly impossible to track with no signal.

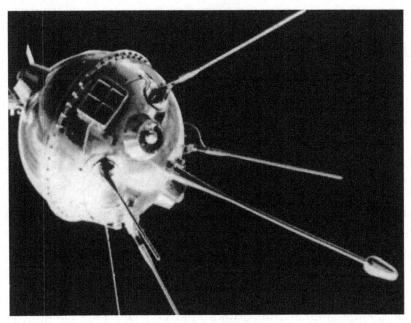

Luna 1 (https://earthsky.org/upl/2012/12/luna-1.jpg)

The Soviet Union would successfully launch two more satellites as a part of the Luna satellite series in 1959. *Luna 2* was the first artificial object to land on the moon, and *Luna 3* successfully returned pictures of the dark side of the moon (the side that we cannot see on Earth).

In 1960, the Soviet Union continued its successful launches, making just two that year. However, the Soviets managed to achieve another major first on August 19, 1960, when they launched *Sputnik 5* into space. This was something that worked toward their longer-term goal of successfully getting a person into space and then back home. Instead of sending just one animal, though, they had what seems more of a menagerie aboard *Sputnik 5*. The passengers on this trip included fruit flies, a rabbit, a pair of rats, forty mice, and plants. However, it was the pair of dogs—named Belka and Strelka—that received the most attention, particularly when they returned to Earth safely. This launch was more like a test run for what was to come, and it was the last major launch before the

Soviets moved onto the next major goal—launching a person into space and returning that person safely back to the ground.

Over time, Belka and Strelka became pop culture icons, inspiring music, cartoons (they were the inspiration for the 1990s cartoon *Ren & Stimpy*), and movies. Strelka had a puppy that was given to Khrushchev, who then gifted the dog to the US First Lady Jacqueline Kennedy. While there was a rivalry between the two nations, the US was the only other country that could understand the pressures of the Space Race, creating strong respect between the two nations that largely directed the path of humanity for several decades. Among many tense exchanges and the Cold War nearing the brink of nuclear war on several occasions, these friendly gestures helped improve the relationship between the two superpowers and set the rest of the world at ease.

The Studies, Failures, and Accomplishments of the US

The US was working toward getting a man into space, but it was also diligent about conducting scientific experiments. From the early days of the agency, it had stated its dedication to launching a pilot into orbit in as short a time as was possible. However, over 1958, the US would have more failed attempts than successes, showing the nation had a long road before it could consider launching a person safely into space. In 1959, US satellites continued to focus on furthering science, even as the Soviet Union continued to collect a string of firsts. Perhaps the constant drive to achieve more came at the cost of getting things right. As the USSR was in a position to be the leader, it had more time, which could have caused the US to push when it wasn't necessarily ready. However, each of these failures provided valuable lessons that the US used to improve its devices and technology.

With a heavy focus on studying space, the US was gaining details about space that would help it create a more reliable rocket.

Other Nations Join in the Race

The Space Race usually refers to the competition between the USSR and the US, but other nations began to join them in sending satellites into space during the 1960s. The UK sent its first satellite into space on April 26th, 1962. The primary objective for its satellite was to gain more data about the relationships of the ionosphere and sun-ionosphere. Canada sent its first satellite, *Alouette* (skylark), into space on September 29, 1962. It was the first satellite to be built by a nation other than the two superpowers. Its primary purpose was also to study the ionosphere. Both the UK and Canada had responded to the US invitation (or more accurately, NASA's invitation) to join an international collaboration to learn about space. Joining the collaboration enabled both nations to use American rockets so that they did not have to develop their own, which the US and USSR had already shown was far more difficult than often anticipated.

Italy joined the collaboration in 1964, and France in 1965, both with their own successful satellites. Australia would send its first satellite from Australia in 1967 with the use of a US rocket. Nations would continue to collaborate, sending their own satellites into space. The decade would close with West Germany finally joining with its own satellite—and a much wider goal than that of previous satellites.

Chapter 8 – The First Men in Space

After spending several years testing in space and learning as much as possible with scientific instruments and short trips using animals, both sides were getting closer to achieve one of the greatest accomplishments in human history—the successful launch of a person into—and back from—space. Both superpowers were eager to be the first, though they went about it in different ways.

The USSR would just barely beat the US to this milestone, with both hitting this goal in 1961.

Yuri Gagarin and a Question of What Counted as a Success

As its technology continued to advance, the Soviet Union started to review potential candidates for the first person in space. The Soviets had narrowed down their options to twenty potential candidates, whom they called cosmonauts. Each of the candidates was required to complete a series of tests to determine their ability to withstand the potential risks. The tests were once described by Cathleen Lewis: "They were performing enormous feats of physical training ... They wanted to test the limits of their pilots." The Soviets had learned from the other missions with animals that it was nearly impossible to guess what would happen once the launch began.

Two men stood out from the other candidates. Twenty-seven-year-old Yuri Gagarin was chosen to be the first Soviet (and, they hoped, person) in space, and Gherman Titov would be his backup. Reportedly, Gagarin had more humble origins, and this was desirable considering what they hoped he would become if the mission was successful. Titov had been raised in a family that was considered middle-class, while Gagarin's parents had been closer to blue-collar workers. This meant he had to overcome more to gain his place, which better represented what the Soviets wanted to portray—a person overcoming much longer odds to become a national hero. It would help inspire people across the Soviet Union to strive for more by working harder.

His humble background could have been a reason, but many people say it was more likely Gagarin's performance during the tests that ultimately led to his being chosen. Unaware that the US had been tracking its own countdown to launch someone into space, the Soviets pushed forward with its own plans in secret. Despite not knowing the American plans, the Soviets were aware that the US was making advances, and they were worried that they would lose the edge they had established through the first round of milestones. To ensure they were the first, the Soviets continued to push for a launch as soon as possible.

Following the rigorous selection process and testing, the USSR began to prepare for the launch, setting up *Vostok 1* on the launchpad. On April 12, 1961, Gagarin prepared himself at the top of a thirty-meter-high booster on the launch site in Kazakhstan (the modern-day Baikonur Cosmodrome). The cosmonaut was five-foot-two-inches tall, which made him a much better choice for the small quarters. Still, it couldn't have been terribly comfortable, as the rocket began to shake before departing from Earth. At 9:07

a.m., he uttered, "Poyekhali," or "Here we go," as the rocket roared to life and launched him into the air.

Previous launches with animals had not told the Soviets what happened once the animals were in space. It was possible that the force of leaving Earth could cause him to lose consciousness. Because of this, they planned for mission control to assume control over the capsule. If he was awake as he orbited the Earth, Gagarin was given tubes with food that he could eat. There was also a ten-day supply of provisions in the event that something went wrong and the mission went longer than the single orbit that was planned. He was also able to relay his current experience back to ground control. The existing transcript from the mission had him reporting back how beautiful the Earth looked as he viewed it from the window of the little capsule. He could see how the shadows cast by clouds appeared from above the clouds. During this time, he was weightless, so Gagarin was also able to report back how he felt, proving that zero-g did not have any obvious adverse effect on a person's cognitive abilities.

A serious risk that was considered prior to his departure was what would happen if he were to lose contact with ground control, and with it, control of the vessel. To address this, NASA provided codes that would allow the cosmonaut to take control should he be disconnected. The capsule included a very crude computer that would allow him to maneuver the vessel.

Following the successful launch, Gagarin and the *Vostok 1* spent 108 minutes orbiting the Earth. They passed once around the planet, roughly 203 miles above the surface. Control then moved the vessel into what was likely a scary descent back to the ground. It is thought in such a controlled fall from space, the pull of gravity Gagarin likely felt was eight times greater than what we experience on the surface. His landing was completely up to the people controlling the vessel, and their control was minimal at best. He was in free fall until he was roughly four miles above the Earth. Then, he ejected from the capsule and parachuted back to the ground.

Some people have questioned whether the record is valid because Gagarin could not land his craft. This is based on the definition of success established by the Fédération Aéronautique Internationale (FAI), which has been the regulatory federation for air sports since 1905. The definition for a successful space flight was based on their regulations from aviation, which stated that the pilot must be able to land the ship. The USSR had not established a reliable way of braking upon reentry (they already had so many other variables to work with that this was not nearly as important). The Vostok craft had no braking mechanism since it was essentially a ballistic craft and followed the same kind of trajectory. Gagarin was ejected because there was no way for him to land safely at the speeds the craft was going. When Gherman Titov became the second person in space, he admitted that he had been ejected from his craft. Up to this point, it was thought that Gagarin had landed his craft, so this information started another controversy. Ultimately, the FAI had to recognize that there was an extremely different set of requirements for space travel than for regular flying. The speed, weight, and other elements of space travel meant that it needed a different definition of what was considered a success. It wasn't the landing that mattered. The fact remains that Gagarin was the first person to go into space and return to Earth to talk about his experience.

Following this success, Gagarin became one of the most notable heroes of the USSR. In March 1968, Gagarin and another pilot died while testing a new fighter jet. Though he did not live long after this first successful mission, he is still honored by people in Russian today, and his reputation wasn't restricted to the USSR. His face and name were plastered on newspapers across the world as the first person to ever enter space, and he lived to tell people just what he saw during his brief visit. When *Apollo 11* landed on the moon in

1969, the crew left a commemorative medallion for Gagarin, even though he did not die during a space mission. It was impossible to overstate just how important this first mission was. The *Apollo 11* crew also left medallions for others who had died in the pursuit of furthering space exploration.

Alan Shepard

Soon after NASA formed, they issued an invitation to 110 test pilots to become volunteers for the new spaceflight program. Alan Shepard was one of those original 110 pilots, but his invitation had gone astray, so he did not receive it. NASA managed to let him know, and he became one of the first seven men to become astronauts. From this group, Shepard was selected to be what NASA hoped would be the first person in space. His backup was John Glenn.

Project Mercury was meant to get the first person into space, and NASA spent several missions running tests with unmanned craft. On April 15, 1961, NASA and the US learned of the successful flight of Yuri Gagarin and realized they had missed their milestone. At best, Alan Shepard would be the first American in space and the second human to reach space. The US was incredibly close to having reached this milestone, so this was a blow to their hopes. The weather would further hinder their progress as the launch of *Mercury 7* was postponed from May 2nd due to weather conditions. It was again postponed because of the weather. On May 5, 1961 (less than a month after the Soviet's success), *Mercury 7* launched with Shepard aboard. After reaching 116 miles above the Earth's surface, Shepard remained in space for fifteen minutes. He did not get a chance to feel weightlessness because NASA had designed the craft so that he was strapped in too tightly to float. He also wasn't able to see the beauty of space because of where the porthole was located. Shepard did have a periscope so he could look outside, but it had a filter that made everything outside look black and white, including Earth.

While the Soviets had achieved the first human flight into space and a full orbit of the planet, *Mercury 7*'s flight gained attention because NASA was so open about its programs. Shepard's launch was televised to the world, and his return to Earth was also broadcasted live. Everyone knew that Gagarin had been the first person in space, but Shepard became a more easily identifiable space traveler because millions saw his trip. This created a connection with him that was not present with Gagarin. In fact, very little about what Gagarin experienced was detailed beyond the fact that he had successfully gone into space and returned.

Upon his return, Shepard was awarded the NASA Distinguished Service Medal, presented by President Kennedy. For the next few Mercury missions, Shepard continued to train, with his next planned flight on *Mercury 10*. However, this mission was scrapped following the successful full-day orbit by Gordon Cooper. Believing they didn't need to continue to test how people reacted to being in space, NASA switched over to the next phase, Project Gemini.

Shepard was designated to be one of the members of the first manned Gemini craft, but during training, he started to feel ill. Off-balance, dizzy, and nauseated, he reported to the physician. He was tested and diagnosed with Ménière's disease, which causes a buildup of fluid in the inner ear. Following the diagnosis, he was grounded from any solo jet test flights and told he could not go into space in 1963. For the next few years, he became NASA's Chief of the Astronaut Office, in charge of managing the astronauts.

Despite still being a part of the project, Shepard missed the potential to fly, as he underwent an operation in 1969 to correct his condition. The operation was successful, and he was reinstated into the program as an astronaut. His first assigned mission was the notorious *Apollo 13*, but he and his crew were pushed back to *Apollo 14* to give them more time to train. Following the problems with *Apollo 13*, NASA made changes to the craft, and Shepard and the crew of *Apollo 14* greatly benefited. During his first and only trip to the moon, Shepard got to play golf on the moon's surface. He and his crew member, Ed Mitchell, spent nine hours and seventeen minutes exploring and playing on the moon. After being away for thirty-three hours, Shepard and Mitchell returned to the craft, where Stuart Roosa had remained.

Shepard became one of a very small number of people to walk on the moon during the 20th century, and, at forty-seven years old, he had the distinction of being the oldest astronaut active with NASA. Shepard had two successful trips into space, logging nearly 217 hours in space. He returned to his role of managing the astronauts after his trip to the moon and finally retired in 1974. However, he continued to work, joining with other Mercury astronauts to start the Mercury Seven Foundation. This foundation was later called the Astronaut Scholarship Foundation, and today it helps fund college students studying a range of sciences and engineering. Shepard was later diagnosed with leukemia and died from complications of the illness in 1998.

The gap between when the Soviet Union achieved a milestone and when the US met that same milestone was closing. It took more than three months after *Sputnik 1* for the US to successfully launch *Explorer 1* into space. Less than three weeks after Gagarin became the first man in space, Shepard became the second.

Other Early Successful Trips

Just ten weeks after Shepard's launch into space, NASA prepared *Mercury 8*, which launched astronaut Virgil Ivan "Gus" Grissom into space on July 21, 1961. His time in space was comparable to Shepard's visit, lasting fifteen minutes. The craft had been adjusted, so Grissom was able to see Earth during his trip, and this wasn't the only change NASA made to the capsule: they changed the way the hatch would open after he splashed down in the ocean. There were several steps that had to be completed for the hatch to open, and it was this series of steps that would become a problem for Grissom.

Unlike Shepard's trip, when Grissom's capsule splashed down in the Atlantic Ocean, the capsule door opened prematurely. He had completed several of the steps, leaving the last one until the helicopter had appeared. Although he hadn't completed the full process, the door opened, and the capsule began to take on water and to sink. With no other choice, Grissom climbed out of the capsule in his spacesuit, which weighed more than twenty pounds. Astronauts spacesuits were designed to float, but this capability required certain steps to prepare—which Grissom did not have time to do before the capsule sank. As he treaded water, the suit began to fill up. It took five minutes before he was finally picked up, ending the struggle to survive. The recovery team did not realize that there was an issue because they had seen how buoyant the suites were. Believing him to be safe, they first moved to retrieve the capsule as it began to sink. As they struggled to pull out the water-filled craft, Grissom was left to try to remain afloat in his increasingly heavy suit.

Some of the recovery team said that Grissom worked to help with the craft recovery. Instead of swimming away from it, he put himself at further risk by remaining close to it. If the craft had sunk, it would have dragged Grissom down with it. Despite the situation, he directed the recovery efforts from his place near the capsule. When the craft was secured, he gave the recovery team two thumbs up to let them know they could start to pull it out of the water. At this point, the recovery team was almost entirely focused on retrieving the ship, so they failed to notice that Grissom himself was in danger. Grissom watched as they successfully lifted the capsule out of the water and water begin to spill out of it. A few waves quickly refilled the capsule, though, and they had to cut it loose.

A second helicopter came to retrieve Grissom only to notice that he was slipping under water. In a hurry to slip into the collar used to retrieve him, Grissom put it on backward but signaled for the crew to pull him up anyway.

The incident has spawned controversy, with some people saying that Grissom panicked and opened the door before he should have. This version was portrayed by Tom Wolfe, who described it as "screwing the pooch." Based on talks with people within NASA, however, Grissom was reacting to a calculated risk NASA had made. Rather than panicking, Grissom had been a quick-thinking hero who had almost single-handedly saved the space program with his actions. The door opening was not his fault; he was simply reacting to a dire situation instead of freezing up and likely dying inside the capsule when it sank. The checklist that was established for opening the hatch was more of a guideline because the process had not been tested after a flight. Grissom was the first to go through it and had not been trained on the new mechanisms. Those who worked closely with him, as well as the senior NASA managers, believed he had acted appropriately for his situation.

Today, NASA would use this as a sign that things needed to be changed. In 1961, this was not an option because of the Space Race. Instead of being hailed a hero like Shepard, Grissom was the first American to have to justify and face scrutiny for his actions. After this, he would spend much of the rest of his career under a cloud.

Because of his fast thinking and quick reaction, Grissom could be credited with helping to keep the program going. About two months before his trip, President Kennedy had announced the intention to get a person on the moon. Had Grissom died, it would have given the president reason to reconsider and potentially slow the project. Grissom became dedicated to making sure things went right after that, and he spent a lot of time learning how the Gemini worked when NASA switched to the second program. He became the first person to make a second trip into space.

Grissom's tenacity and dedication earned him considerable respect within NASA, and he was chosen to be the captain of the three-member crew of *Apollo 1*. He and the other two crew members, Edward White and Roger Chaffee, died when the oxygen-rich capsule caught fire during a rehearsal. Some of the senior members of NASA have since admitted that had he lived, Grissom would have been their choice to be the first man on the moon since he had been in the program longer than anyone else.

Soon after Grissom's successful trip to space, Gherman Titov became the second Soviet to enter space, and he spent far longer in space than Gagarin. Both Soviets had managed to accomplish more than the short trips completed by the astronauts.

Titov was one of the finalists to be the first man in space, but there were good reasons why he was not ultimately chosen for the distinction. Unlike Gagarin, Titov had a temper that had gotten him into trouble on a few occasions (some even say it was one of the reasons he was not selected to be the first cosmonaut in space). It was said that he and Gagarin clashed, largely because of Titov's temper. Only slightly taller than Gagarin, at five-foot four inches, he was still small enough to fit into the capsule, yet his study build and athletic history made him ideal for the second trip, which would be considerably longer than a single trip around the Earth.

Titov himself would later indicate that he agreed with the choice to send Gagarin into space first, especially since the first man in space would spend a lot of time traveling around the Soviet Union talking to people. According to Titov, "It was Gagarin's character that mattered most. [Yuri] turned out to be the man that everyone loved. Me, they couldn't love ... I'm not lovable. I have a very explosive character. I could easily say rude things, offend someone, and walk away. I wasn't a very convenient person for the leadership; I had my own opinion about things and knew how to insist on things. This did not always stir up warm feelings ... but Yuri could talk freely to anyone— he could speak their language. The first man in space had to be a nice, attractive person ... they were right to choose [Yuri]."

Titov's flight was the second for the Soviet Union, but he was the fourth person into space (Shepard and Gus Grissom had both gone into space by the time he launched). He took off on August 6, 1961, becoming only the second person to orbit the Earth. He was the first person to spend more than a day in space, with his mission lasting twenty-five hours and eighteen minutes. He returned to Earth and became another Soviet hero.

He would later have another first that is far less known. A few months before his flight, Titov and his wife lost a baby son because of a heart defect. A few years after his trip into space, they would have a healthy daughter, making her the first child who was born to a person who had gone into space. He did not return to space, instead becoming a deputy of the Supreme Soviet. When the Soviet Union ended in 1991, he moved into politics, voted into the Russian parliament in 1995. He died in 2000.

John Glenn was one of the original seven astronauts in Project Mercury. On February 20, 1962, he became the fifth person in space and the first American to fully orbit the Earth. Three women working with computers back at NASA ensure his trip was a success: Mary Jackson, Dorothy Vaughan, and Katherine Johnson. Like Shepard, Glenn became an immediate American hero. His mission lasted four hours and fifty-five minutes. He would also utter one of the most famous quotes about what it was like to be one of the first people in space: "I felt exactly how you would feel if you were getting ready to launch and knew you were sitting on top of two million parts—all built by the lowest bidder on a government contract." It was perhaps as close as any of the astronauts came to criticizing NASA, but was certainly a fair critic of their situation. The men were already putting their lives on the line to see what was possible, while the government chose contracts that would help them keep the budget from continuing to balloon. This would prove to be something that would later come back to haunt NASA in the 1980s.

Glenn retired from space travel in 1964, but he would not stay away for long. In 1974, he was elected to the US Senate, serving as a senator for Ohio. He would be repeatedly elected to serve in the Senate, and he became one of the Senate's leading experts in science and technology. He retired from the Senate in 1997. The next year, he returned to space, making him the oldest person to go into space at that time. During the flight, he helped to study the aging process, spending longer in space during this last trip than his previous visit—a total of nine days. Glenn died in 2016, making him the last of the original astronauts to pass.

First Woman in Space

While NASA debated about adding women to the astronaut rosters (something the men in the program seem to have opposed: Glenn made a speech that largely said it wasn't the woman's role in American society), the USSR had far fewer problems with the concept of women participating in the Space Race.

Due to this difference, the Soviets quickly earned distinction for putting the first woman into space two decades before the US did. Inspired by Gagarin's trip into space, Valentina Tereshkova joined the cosmonaut program. While she had no experience as a pilot, she had been an active member of the Yaroslavl Air Sports Club and completed 126 successful parachute jumps. Since cosmonauts were ejected from their capsules, this made her an ideal candidate. She and four other women underwent eighteen months of training very similar to what the men went through.

Chosen to be the pilot of *Vostok 6*, Tereshkova was the only woman of the five to make the trip into space on June 16, 1963, two days after Valery Bykovsky was sent into space in *Vostok 5*. The pair conducted different orbits and passed close to each other, testing communications as they passed. Her image and time in the capsule were broadcast back to the USSR as she logged over seventy hours and nearly fifty rotations around the Earth.

During her time in space, there was a problem with the automatic navigation software, causing her craft to start moving away from the planet. When she noticed, she received a new set of algorithms from the scientists back on Earth. She returned safely, close to the Kazakhstan-Mongolian-Chinese border. Her face was bruised, but she was otherwise unharmed. Instead of going for the required medical tests, she went with the recovery team to get dinner first, something that earned her a reprimand.

Though few knew of the near disaster, Valentina was hailed as a hero. Like Gagarin, she would become a spokesperson for the Soviets. Though she didn't return to space, she did become a test pilot and earned a doctorate. In 1963, she married another cosmonaut, Andriyan Nikolayev. They became the first couple in human history to have both gone into space and then have a child together. Their daughter received attention from the medical field because of this, and later, she herself became a doctor.

Tereshkova had continued to talk about her time in space and became a member of the effort for cooperation in space travel with other nations. She is still alive and an active member of the space community.

Chapter 9 – JFK's Resolve and Prediction of the Ultimate Win – Reaching the Moon

In the early 1960s, the Space Race was heating up as the two nations managed to send people into space. On September 12, 1962, President John F. Kennedy delivered a speech to stir the American people's emotions and enthusiasm for the efforts to travel in space. Known today as the "Moon Speech," this oratory helped bring more focus to the American effort in space exploration, which had lost some luster since the Soviets continually beat the US to major milestones.

Speaking in front of a crowd at Rice University in Houston, Texas, the president focused not on what had happened (Shepard, Grissom, and Glenn had all successfully gone into space, but the Soviets had done more with their two, who both orbited the Earth), but on what he wanted to happen. He had first talked about going to the moon the year before, but the USSR had repeatedly done more since that time. By refocusing the country's efforts on what was possible, he inspired more people to support the program. Kennedy didn't just state the plan to put a man on the moon—he made it an American objective that received the funding it needed to ensure it was achieved before the close of the decade.

The speech was a part of a larger tour that included a visit to Houston, Florida, and Alabama (three key locations for NASA's work). With people beginning to question why the US was involved in the race, Kennedy emphasized that it wasn't just about beating the Soviets, but about pushing boundaries as a part of the American dream. To a crowd of about 40,000 people, he spoke some of the words he is best known for uttering during his presidency:

> For the eyes of the world now look into space, to the moon and to the planets beyond, and we have vowed that we shall not see it governed by a hostile flag of conquest, but by a banner of freedom and peace. We have vowed that we shall not see space filled with weapons of mass destruction, but with instruments of knowledge and understanding.
>
> Yet the vows of this nation can only be fulfilled if we in this nation are first, and, therefore, we intend to be first. In short, our leadership in science and in industry, our hopes for peace and security, our obligations to ourselves as well as others, all require us to make this effort, to solve these mysteries, to solve them for the good of all men, and to become the world's leading space-faring nation.
>
> We choose to go to the moon. We choose to go to the moon in this decade and do the other things, not because they are easy, but because they are hard, because that goal will serve to organize and measure the best of our energies and skills, because that challenge is one that we are willing to accept, one we are unwilling to postpone, and one which we intend to win, and the others, too.
>
> - *President John F. Kennedy*

His argument was that space travel was inevitable. If the US did not continue to push forward, the Soviets would gain the upper hand, making space far more hostile (the Soviets had a similar concern if the US gained the upper hand). By abdicating that lead, the US was failing in its responsibilities to use its technology and abilities to their fullest extent.

One reason Kennedy did not focus on the past but rather set this ambitious goal was that it was an area in which the Soviets did not already have a substantial head start. With Gagarin becoming the first person in space, the US needed a longer-range goal that would give the country a good chance of succeeding first. Kennedy and his administration consulted with their best scientist, von Braun, to see what was realistic. Von Braun said that the best sporting chance the US had was with the goal of reaching the moon. The US had bigger capsules, which gave it a lead over the USSR.

The speech set an incredibly difficult goal, but it had originally included a shorter timeframe: he was supposed to announce the goal of landing on the moon by 1967. This would have been a way of noting the 50th anniversary of the Bolshevik Revolution and could have helped to push the Soviets to agree to engage in the challenge that the president had issued. Fortunately, Kennedy realized before he started his speech that the timelines was perhaps too ambitious and changed the wording so that it simply said by the end of the decade.

Kennedy was assassinated a few years later, but his vision was realized as Americans would be the first on the moon (the Soviets never succeeded in orbiting the moon, let alone landing on it), and they would reach this major milestone in 1969 before the decade ended.

His words still resonate today, though for different reasons. NASA's funding would start to be reduced after the

US had shown its dominance in space, but any efforts to close parts of the agency have been easily denied. This is largely because space still inspires people to do more. Some even credit the speech with pushing the US to meet the goal expressed by a president who was killed in office. Money poured into Project Apollo, and it is estimated that the full project cost $25 billion (an estimated $100 billion today with inflation). Though some experts believe people would have inevitably walked on the moon, even they think it could have taken decades. Given how quickly funding into NASA cooled after Apollo's success, it's also possible the milestone may not have been met as quickly without Kennedy's rousing speech.

What is certain is that without the speech and the Space Race, the push to get to the moon would have been much weaker and would have likely remained only within a small community. As it was, Kennedy made it a point of national pride and interest that gave Americans a common goal and a set timeline by which to accomplish it.

Chapter 10 – The Three Primary NASA Programs

Because of the secretive nature of the Soviet's space program, it is far more difficult to dive into the details of their work. They did keep documents of their progress, but many of them were only released at the end of the 20th century and early 21st century. NASA was far more open about their work because the US wanted to make space exploration an international effort. They did keep some elements secret, particularly the technology used to achieve some of their most impressive feats, but they published a considerable amount of information about their primary projects. Unlike the USSR, space exploration in the US was established to be something for everyone, not just the military. There was a crossover between the technology and knowledge applied to space travel and used in the military (and astronauts were often selected from military pilots), but much of what the US learned was shared with the world.

The three primary projects that NASA established are well-documented within the media and archives, giving people a way to look back at how they were received and what kinds of expectations were established for each of them.

Project Mercury – 1961 until 1963

One thing no one knew at the beginning of 1961 was if it was even possible to send someone into space. It was known that Laika had survived for a while in space (most of the world was still under the impression she had survived for most of the orbits), but that didn't necessarily mean it would be possible for a person to withstand the same experience based on what a person requires compared to a dog, particularly in terms of oxygen. Since the USSR provided not real information with their announcement, the US had no idea just what to expect from the launch of a larger animal into space, let alone what would happen to a person. This would serve as the first obvious goal for the US, followed by information on how they could sustain life for longer periods of time. They would take a very measured approach to accomplish this, setting the stage for how the other two projects would be set up.

The primary objective of Project Mercury was to assess if humans could withstand the experience, what was needed to sustain human life in space, and to begin understanding what could be accomplished. At this point, they weren't sure that a trip to the moon was possible. The early Mercury missions focused on sending a single person into space using vessels that were specifically designed for the project. However, there was room to cut the project short in the event that they were able to accomplish the primary objective early. Project Mercury was as much about establishing a realistic pace for what was possible and safe as it was about beating the Soviets. After all, there had been enough of an uproar among other nations following Laika's death that the US did not want to potentially face backlash from not completing its due diligence. They would also learn through this project just how expensive it was to train and prepare people for the trip into space.

Project Mercury had six missions, with the astronauts spending a total of thirty-four hours over the Earth. Shepard's mission was part of the Mercury project. Inspired by the success of the launch,

Kennedy announced the intent of getting a man on the moon before the end of the decade. With more funds appropriated to the effort, NASA started planning to meet the goal of landing people on the moon. This did not mean that Project Mercury ended. NASA continued to send astronauts into space for brief periods to learn more about what people would need while orbiting in space.

Project Gemini – 1965 until 1966

Project Gemini built on the successful launches from Project Mercury. The first two launches (April 8, 1964 and January 19, 1965) were test missions and did not have crews. The first mission with a crew launched March 23, 1965, and returned to Earth the same day.

NASA used Gemini to learn more about what was possible in space. They tested how to maneuver in space, change orbit, dock with a rocket (they would need to dock with the main vehicle after reaching the moon's surface), and spend some time in space. All these activities were necessary for achieving the long-term goal of walking on the moon. The last mission, Gemini 12, included Jim Lovell and Buzz Aldrin and lasted from November 11, 1966, to November 15, 1966. Returning both men safely, NASA proved it could support life in space for more than just a short trip.

The longest mission had been that of *Gemini 7*, with a launch on December 4, 1965 and splashdown on December 18, 1965. The crew, Frank Borman and Jim Lovell, had spent two weeks in space. It was not known how long it would take to get a manned craft to the moon, so this trip showed NASA that it had the ability to sustain people for longer trips into space.

During all the missions, the crews had worked and done regular daily tasks. The cumulative results of each mission assured NASA it had its bases covered to plan a trip to the moon. Its scientists would be able to provide an environment in which astronauts could live and work for the duration of the trip to the moon, and the team had learned how to maneuver crafts in space, dock, and walk in space.

Project Apollo – 1967 until 1972

Easily the most famous of NASA's projects, Apollo was the one that finally saw the ultimate milestone – people walking on the moon and coming home safely. The project began with tragedy when the crew of *Apollo 1* was killed by fire in the oxygen-rich environment. Because of this tragedy, modifications were made to the cabin and craft.

Unmanned crafts were also tested. The first crew to enter space as a part of Project Apollo reached the moon's orbit, behind when the Soviets had reached the celestial object with their satellites. This was when the US really started to pull ahead in the Space Race, a position they retained over the rest of the competition. *Apollo 8* launched on December 21, 1968, and marked the first time the US had clearly taken the lead in the Space Race. The Soviet Union had reached the moon with *Luna 2*, but with several competing teams within the space program following Korolev's death, the focus was more on outperforming each other than beating the US. While the USSR contended with infighting, NASA continued to push the Apollo project, which completed two more successful missions to orbit the moon. During these missions, the lunar module was tested to see if astronauts could dock and undock to the main craft. *Apollo 11* would be the mission and spacecraft that made history with the first two people to walk on the moon.

Following the success of *Apollo 11*, NASA completed six more missions with varying degrees of success. Each mission purposed to have its teams visit and study different parts of the moon. After *Apollo 11*, the *Apollo 13* mission is probably the next most famous, as an explosion prevented the crew from reaching the moon. While the primary objective was a failure, NASA proved its ability to overcome the unexpected and resolve crises. The team still went around the moon and returned home safely, inspiring the movie, *Apollo 13*, several decades later.

The last mission was *Apollo 17*, launching on December 11, 1972, and returning December 19, 1972. Six Apollo missions successfully landed on the moon, and significant data was collected during these trips. The crews returned with rocks, dirt, and other things from the moon's surface, totaling about 880 pounds of samples.

Chapter 11 – The First Spacewalks

With both the USSR and US working to be the first on the moon, there were many other firsts. One milestone would be critical for any real time in space: the ability to safely spacewalk. If anything happened to the spacecraft, people would need to be able to safely exit and make repairs. It was also necessary to know how people would react to space since they would be exposed to it on the moon's surface. Both sides needed to determine how to design spacesuits that would allow people to survive outside the controlled environment of their space capsules.

The Soviets were the first to successfully complete a spacewalk. On March 18, 1965, cosmonaut Alexei Leonov exited his *Voskhod 2* and spent twelve minutes outside the craft. There were many things no one could have known about being outside of the protection of a spacecraft, and Leonov would be uncomfortable. Some who analyzed the data from his experience described it as miserable. As he floated in open space, his temperature rose sharply, putting him at risk of heatstroke. Outside the protection of *Voskhod 2*, he was exposed to the vacuum of space, which caused issues no one had anticipated. His spacesuit expanded, so when he headed back to the hatch to reenter the vessel, he had to exert himself—something that was difficult since he was already close to overheating. Having reentered *Voskhod 2*, Leonov returned safely to Earth. He would later relate that the sound he most remembered was the sound of his own breathing, which he described as labored.

Since the Soviets did not share much of what they learned, the US would largely learn about the dangers of space on its own. However, it had also collected much more data to better plan for the possible conditions. Therefore, its spacesuits would not have the kinds of problems Leonov experienced. A few months after the Soviet spacewalk, NASA sent Edward White into space to conduct the first American spacewalk on June 3, 1965. This was part of the *Gemini IV* mission, and it proved to be a very different experience for the American. Remaining in space for nearly twice as long, at twenty-three minutes, White reportedly said, "I feel like a million dollars." His tasks were also far different: instead of remaining still in space, he had a hand-held zip gun, which he used to move around. Like many other US missions, this was televised, so the recording of White using the little zip gun to enjoy his experience can still be watched today. When the gun ran out of fuel, he was basically done. As he returned, one of the extra gloves floated out of the open hatch. Knowing he had to return to the ship, White was reported to have called the end of his time in space "... the saddest moment of my life."

The next spacewalk happened on June 5, 1966, when Eugene Cernan was given a chance to leave the vessel during the *Gemini 9* mission. Given White's reaction, most people thought Cernan would have as much fun, particularly as he was given a backpack to help him maneuver. The backpack was located outside of the craft, though, meaning that Cernan had to go retrieve it. Without any means of controlling his motions to reach it, the astronaut had to move towards it using the few handholds on the ship. Consequently, he was spun around. The uncontrollable motions, coupled with the risky task, caused his heart rate to increase to 155 beats per minute. His visor became so foggy he could no longer see. Though his spacesuit size was not a problem, his near blindness made it even harder for him to reenter the craft than what Leonov had experienced. Cernan did not enjoy the experience, comparing it to trying to put a cork back into a champagne bottle.

Buzz Aldrin would be the last American to walk in space before the US reached the moon. His trip was on November 13, 1966, rounding out the spacewalks for Project Gemini. During this mission, Aldrin would leave the craft several times. His was the longest spacewalk, lasting two hours as he moved around the outside of the craft on a tether, taking pictures and looking at the world. He added to a map of the stars and collected some micrometeorite samples. In total, Aldrin spent nearly five and a half hours in space between the three trips in and out of the craft.

The Soviet's next successful spacewalk was in January of 1969 and involved two cosmonauts spacewalking at the same time. Boris Volynov was the commander who stayed on the *Soyuz 5*. Aleksei Yeliseyev and Yevgeny Khrunov left the vessel to board *Soyuz 4*, which was commanded by Vladimir Shatalov. The two men successfully transferred to the other vessel, though there was a problem when Volynov reentered Earth. He survived but lost some teeth when he was tossed across *Soyuz 5*'s cockpit.

Chapter 12 – The First Successful Spacecraft Docking

One of the last major hurdles to reaching the moon was the ability to dock in space since no vehicle could be sent directly to the moon. As this was impossible to replicate on Earth, it became one of the last major missions of Project Gemini. On March 16, 1966, *Gemini 8* launched from Cape Canaveral, Florida. Aboard the craft were Neil Armstrong and David Scott, who would be in space for three days to complete several tasks. The primary objective was for the two men to complete a series of four docking tests. This was a necessary step in finally reaching the moon as NASA was working on the Lunar Module. The craft that the astronauts would be in as they went to the moon was not meant to land on its surface. Instead, the Lunar Module would be used by the two people who would walk on the moon. After leaving the moon, the astronauts would need to dock with the main craft before starting the return trip to Earth.

There had been two earlier Gemini missions (6 and 7) in which the crew had successfully rendezvoused in space but had not attempted to dock. This was one milestone the US achieved first in a series of first that increasingly went to the capitalist nation, particularly after the main Soviet scientist, Korolev, died in 1966. Without him, the Soviets would fall behind as members of their space teams vied for control and competed against each other. Korolev had largely been their unifying leader, which became clear after his passing.

During the Gemini mission, Scott was scheduled to complete several extra-vehicular activities (EVA), which would build on White's spacewalk the previous year. Armstrong was in command, and after they had completed five orbits in six hours, he moved the craft toward Agena-D to begin docking. Scott would later describe the experience, saying they fell silent as they listened for signs that the docking was going as planned. Armstrong and Scott heard their first contact with the target vessel, followed by the unmistakable sound of the latches locking into place. They said it was surprisingly easy.

This early success was quickly disrupted by issues. Before they could celebrate, Scott noticed that the 8-ball the commander had given with them was rolling, which it shouldn't have done in space. To conserve the fuel on the Gemini craft, the crew had used the Agena's engine to complete the docking. They turned this off, which momentarily stopped the toy's movement. But then it began to roll faster. The pair were rotating along all three axes (yaw, pitch, and roll). Mission Control had advised them to undock if they had problems, which Armstrong did. Once they were separated, the crew began trying to steady the Gemini. This was when they realized the problem was with *Gemini 8*, not Agena. They would later learn that one of the maneuver systems on the *Gemini 8* had short-circuited and was perpetually firing.

Calling ground control, they reported they were having an issue as Gemini tumbled end over end through space. It's estimated that they were completing a revolution every second, and it was beginning to make both men very dizzy. Thinking quickly,

Armstrong disabled the OAMS thrusters and activated the thrusters at the front of the craft, which helped it to stabilize.

Though they had planned to do a lot more, both men knew that protocol called for them to head home. They did not know what was causing the problem, so they needed to return to have the spacecraft assessed. Despite the problem, they had successfully docked. This mission was a partial success, but having failed to complete all of the initially planned tasks, it was not considered a complete success. They have managed to prove that it was possible—even easy—to dock with another craft without an astronaut having to go outside. This was at least a reliable proof of concept, so NASA was able to move forward with the Gemini Project. Despite the mixed success of the mission, it did end up in the *Guinness World Records* as the first time two craft docked in space. The record does address the fact that the spacewalks were scrapped because the thrusts malfunctioned.

Gemini 10 would successfully complete the rest of the original *Gemini 8* tasks with the crew members John Young and Michael Collins.

In 1967, the Soviets completed the first unmanned docking in space. Then, in January 1969, they would successfully dock with crew members. Since the USSR was the only other country to be working in space at the time, they did get a mention in the *Guinness World Records*, as well. It further mentions that the crew members were able to successfully switch.

Chapter 13 – Apollo 11 – One Small Step for Man

Though the Apollo project started in tragedy, it ultimately gave the US an undeniable lead in the Space Race. The USSR would never catch up to the American accomplishments.

On July 20, 1969, NASA successfully sent a crew to the moon, and two of the three men successfully landed on the surface before later returning.

Planning

Following the disaster and tragedy of *Apollo 1*, NASA waited almost two years for the next manned mission to the moon to ensure that a similar disaster did not happen again. They had lost three men on Earth, and this reminded everyone just how dangerous space exploration was, even before astronauts reached space.

Three men were chosen to crew *Apollo 11*: Commander Neil Armstrong, Buzz Aldrin, and Michael Collins. All the men had a unique history that made them ideal for their respective roles. At thirty-eight-years-old, Armstrong had commanded two missions and was the first civilian to do so. Aldrin, a year older, was the first astronaut to have a doctorate. His intellect made him an ideal choice as the pilot of the Lunar Module. Finally, Collins had successfully walked in space during *Gemini 10.*

Collins was assigned the role of remaining on the Apollo spacecraft while Armstrong and Aldrin would board the Lunar Module and walk on the moon's surface. Prior to the mission, the men had not worked together, but once they were selected, they went through a rigorous training program that lasted six months. All three of them had been in successful missions, but this was their first time working on a mission together.

The Launch and Landing on the Moon

On July 16, 1969, the three-member crew lifted off from Cape Canaveral, Florida, at 9:32 a.m. Cameras were rolling to capture the launch, and the crew filmed themselves twice during their flight. Their third transmission gained far more attention than the other broadcasts because the surface of the moon could be seen from the craft. It took four days, but on July 20, 1969, Armstrong and Aldrin went aboard the Lunar Module, called the "Eagle," and set off for the moon's surface.

Aldrin landed the Eagle in what is called the Sea of Tranquility, a sizeable basaltic region of the moon. Upon their successfully landing, Armstrong reported back to mission control: "Houston, Tranquility Base here. The Eagle has landed." After this, the two men did not rush out the door, as many people today imagine. Instead, they spent two hours doing a comprehensive systems' check, setting them so that the Lunar Module would remain on the moon. They were about to exit a craft without any tether, so they wanted to make sure it didn't drift away or have any problems that would strand them on the moon's surface. They also had a meal.

One Giant Leap for Mankind

After those two hours, the cameras were turned on, and people watched as Armstrong exited the Eagle. At 11:56 p.m., Armstrong made history as he took the first step on the moon and uttered one of the most well-known quotes in human history: "That's one small step for man, one giant leap for mankind." About twenty minutes later, Aldrin's exit from the Eagle was captured by Armstrong from the moon's surface. Images of the time are mostly of Aldrin since, as the commander, Armstrong was responsible for documenting the entire mission and was the one taking the pictures. Given the difficulty of telling the difference between them in their large spacesuits, this is something that often goes unnoticed by people today.

It was not enough for the men to simply land on the moon and return, though. NASA was dedicated to getting as much scientific data as possible from each mission and, considering this was the first time anyone had landed on the moon, there were many tasks Armstrong and Aldrin were expected to complete before returning home. They completed several experiments and collected samples from the moon's surface. One of the most interesting tasks they completed while still on the moon was calling President Richard Nixon.

A somber element was added to the trip as they placed medals on the planet to commemorate astronauts and cosmonauts who had died, including Gagarin and the three crew members of *Apollo 1*. While the Space Race may have caused tensions between the two countries, the people who had been to space felt a sense of comradery that made nationality irrelevant. The competition did not negate what the other nation had accomplished, and those who died in the pursuit of space exploration deserved to be remembered.

Since NASA had worked with scientists from many other nations, a disk that included messages provided by seventy-three countries was left on the moon. The astronauts also left a plaque with the following words:

Here men from the planet earth

First set foot upon the moon

July 1969, A.D.

We came in peace for all mankind

Though there was certainly a sense of international backing, Armstrong and Aldrin planted the US flag on the moon, providing a visible symbol of who had reached the moon first.

During their time on the moon, the two had moved up to 200 feet away from the Eagle when they headed into a crater on the moon's surface. When they left, they took more than forty-five pounds of samples with them. They reported that moving around on the moon's surface was far easier than they had imagined. Armstrong had been out of the craft for about two and a half hours when he reentered the Eagle.

When the Eagle left the moon, it had spent twenty-one and a half hours on the surface, or nearly a full day. At 1:54 p.m., they returned to the *Columbia* with the samples they had collected. This time, Armstrong got to experience a much smoother docking experience. Back on the craft, they began their return to Earth.

On July 24, 1969, at 12:50 p.m., Armstrong and Aldrin splashed down in the Pacific Ocean. They were recovered, then immediately put into isolation suits since it wasn't certain if anything harmful could have returned with them from the moon. Once they had been scrubbed with iodine, they boarded a helicopter to start their trek back to Houston. When they reached Houston, they began quarantine, which lasted until August 10, 1969.

Armstrong largely moved into a more private life. He died on August 25, 2012. Aldrin and Collins continued to speak as members of the Apollo project well into their 80s, and both men were still alive as of 2020.

A Unique Accomplishment

The Soviet Union failed to land on the moon, and more than fifty years later, no other nation besides the US has successfully landed on the moon. The last time the US went to the moon was in 1972. Attempting to travel to the moon now would mean returning to the drawing board because there have been many advances, particularly in terms of digital technology. While some nations are working to land on the moon, there is neither a strong incentive to spur them to action, like the speech delivered by President Kennedy, nor a fierce competition like that between the US and USSR from the 1950s to the 1970s.

The Space Race continued, but it slowed significantly after the final Apollo trip to the moon. Both nations focused on other areas of space travel. The US moved toward developing space shuttles, which would provide a more easily-controlled way of landing after reentering Earth's atmosphere. These craft would not be able to land on the moon. The USSR largely focused on working on satellites, as it was less costly to send unmanned vehicles into space.

Even if it wasn't the end of the Space Race, there were no more inspiring milestones that could compare to the ones up to this point (going to Mars was far beyond the capability of either nation). While there would still be plenty of other firsts both nations achieved, there hasn't been the same amount of interest or dedication of funds since 1972. The modern-day public seems to take it for granted that people can walk on the moon, but it will take a considerable rethinking of how to do it and nearly as many years to accomplish as the amount of time between Kennedy's 1962 speech and the first step Armstrong took in 1969.

Chapter 14 – Those Who Gave Their Lives

All the people who elected to be cosmonauts and astronauts entered their respective programs knowing the risks. What they were doing was comparable to what Europeans had done when they headed to the New World across an ocean. However, unlike those travelers, the people who chose to go into space did so knowing there would be no help if something happened. No ship could come by to save them. Space was an unknown frontier where anything that went wrong would spell death for those aboard their vessels. *Apollo 13* is perhaps the most well-known example of how things could have gone wrong (largely because of the movie it inspired several decades later).

Unfortunately, there were times when people were not successful in escaping death. Given how little was known about space and what conditions were the most stable for human life, there were times when practicing for potential issues and conditions led to the death of astronauts and cosmonauts while still on Earth.

Cosmonauts Who Are Known to Have Perished During Their Duties

Only since the Space Race ended has the USSR (and later Russia) begun to release details about its space program and the number of cosmonauts who died become public knowledge.

While preparing to launch the first person into space, the USSR began training cosmonauts in an oxygen-rich environment. The cosmonaut in the training cabin at the time died in a fire that quickly got out of control. Had the Soviets shared what they learned during this tragedy, other lives could have been saved.

For a long time, the first known cosmonaut to die was Vladimir Komarov. When the *Soyuz 1* parachute was deployed, it failed to open. He plummeted to Earth, dying on April 24, 1967.

While undocking from the Salyut 1 space station, the crew of the *Soyuz 11* headed home on June 30, 1971. Roughly thirty minutes before returning to Earth, one of the key valves presumably opened, causing the cabin to decompress. The three cosmonauts, Georgi Dobrovolski, Vladislav Volkov, and Viktor Patsayev, would have died instantly. When the craft landed, people opened the door and found the three cosmonauts deceased. Until the early 21st century, they were the only three people to die in space.

It is unknown how many cosmonauts perished since the accuracy of the Soviet records is questionable. It is possible that the number of people who are known to have died completing their duties is accurate, but it is also possible that the records were misrepresented, like what was broadcasted about Laika. It took decades before her actual fate became known. Still, the information was eventually released, suggesting there may not be additional deaths.

Astronauts Who Perished

Technically, there are no US astronauts who died in space. That does not mean the nation has a spotless record. More than a few astronauts have perished while training or during different phases of missions.

The first astronaut to die was Theodore Freeman while testing a T-38 on October 31, 1964. During the test, it struck a goose. Parts of the vehicle broke apart and were sucked into the engines. Though he successfully ejected from the vehicle, Freeman was too close to the ground for his parachute to fully deploy, and he died.

Two astronauts, Charles Bassett and Elliot See, the chosen crew members for *Gemini 9*, were killed while aboard a T-38. Another astronaut, Clifton Williams, would also die while aboard a T-38.

As related previously, the original crew of *Apollo 1*, Virgil Grissom, Roger Chaffee, and Edward White, died while training for the mission in Cape Kennedy. NASA had constructed a training exercise in an oxygen-rich environment. As the Soviets had learned a few years earlier, this was a risky environment. When a fire started in the cabin, the astronauts perished before anyone could get to them.

Michael Adams was not officially an astronaut when he went aboard the X-15 on November 15, 1967. The vehicle broke up while he was in flight, killing him. He would be given the title of astronaut posthumously.

Perhaps the most well-known fatal American incident occurred on January 28, 1986. With the Space Race cooling and few new milestones achieved the previous few years, launches had not attracted much attention. But, for the first time, NASA was sending up a civilian. After a long competition, a teacher, Sharon (Christa) McAuliffe, was selected to join six astronauts on the space shuttle *Challenger*. The day of the launch was cold, causing the failure of an O-ring that was a part of the rocket motors. When the motor began to leak exhaust, other parts of the structure began to fail. The shuttle had launched on time, but seventy-three seconds later, as it was going up into the sky, the shuttle exploded. All seven people aboard died:

- Commander Dick Scobee

- Pilot Michael Smith

- Gregory Jarvis (Payload Specialist)

- Judy Resnik (Mission Specialist)

- Ronald McNair (Mission Specialist)

- Ellison Onizuka (Mission Specialist)

- Sharon (Christa) McAuliffe (teacher and first citizen to be selected for space travel)

The Space Race ended in 1991, but others who have died in the pursuit of furthering science in the US. All members aboard the space shuttle *Columbia* perished when the space shuttle disintegrated while returning to Earth. Up to that point, the mission had been successful.

Others Who Died in the Name of Space Exploration

The previous section covered the people who volunteered to go into space knowing the risks, but many other people died while testing equipment and during launches. Like many other scientific fields, space flight holds a significant element of risk for those involved. For example, estimates say between 78 and 160 people were killed when one of the 1960 Soviet launches went very wrong, killing nearly every present, including some higher Soviet officials.

Still, it is a field that inspires and stimulates the imagination. Despite the dangers, it still attracts attention, and people are eager to contribute to space exploration. With as much as the US and USSR accomplished during the Space Race, there are still so many first left to be achieved. Knowing the risks, people are still interested in seeing what they can contribute.

The loss of the brave people who were willing to risk their lives in the name of exploration and scientific advancement is tragic. Nevertheless, both the Soviet and American programs had impressive safety records considering the dangers of space travel, particularly in the early days. As more nations and businesses become interested in seeing what they can achieve, the number of deaths has continued to rise. Just as with aviation, there are simply risks that come with space training and travel. Space travel is still far from being safe enough for commercial flights, but over time, it will hopefully become as reliable as flight.

Chapter 15 – The Long, Bumpy Road to Coordination

Fear of losing technical and military superiority had led both nations to push themselves and their scientists to be superior to the other's. The Space Race helped create two of the most advanced and outstanding programs the world has seen. By the 1980s, the drive for superiority had mostly disappeared. Both nations had spent substantial amounts on their programs. The USSR's program was starting to have problems and stumble, making it difficult to dedicate funds to a project that had not seen any successes as inspirational as those achieved under Korolev.

The US had been pushing for a greater contingent of nations working together for the peaceful advancement of space exploration with the help of the United Nations (UN), which responded by creating a committee dedicated to the cause. Eventually, the USSR would join, though not in the early years. The Committee on Space Research was a similar effort headed by the international scientific community. This committee mandated that both the US and USSR appoint their vice presidents to the committee, with the purpose of starting a dialogue between the two biggest participants in the Space Race. Academician Anatoli Blagonravov was the representative for the USSR. There was a complication with this appointment, though, since the Soviet military insisted on providing its approval before anything was finalized. By comparison, the US had long been working with other nations, with NASA providing a single umbrella for these efforts. As a civilian agency (not a military one), remained focused on science instead of military developments. This meant that NASA could more easily obtain resources, jointly develop ideas within the scientific community, and rethink technology. The Soviet advances made in the early days of the Space Race were unsustainable, and the isolation that the USSR experienced as time pressed on led it to fall behind after the death of Korolev in 1966.

The US and USSR had periodically tried to collaborate since 1960. The Space Race had proved to be a very expensive endeavor, making a collaborative effort desirable for financial reasons. It would also allow them to know what kind of technology each had, which could have alleviated some of the tensions of the Cold War. Eisenhower's initiative, called "Atoms for Peace," nearly brought the two superpowers together as they planned a summit for April of 1960. Unfortunately, the summit was canceled when a US spy plane was shot down over USSR territories.

US President John F. Kennedy would continue to try for a more cooperative approach with the USSR. The day he assumed office, his inaugural address clearly stated this desire. In 1961, he called for this effort to begin: "Let both sides seek to invoke the wonders of science instead of its terrors. Together let us explore the stars." Khrushchev was unmoved by this call, especially as the USSR seemed to be superior in its approach and were already planning to send the first man into space. The Soviet media displayed their superior abilities, giving them no incentive to accept the US's call to work together. The problem with this approach would later be more obvious. The USSR was so focused on accomplishing a range of firsts that it failed to conduct the same levels of scientific research the US had completed with its earliest satellites. The US was not that far behind the Soviet Union in its firsts, while the gap between the nations' understanding of space and meteorological data was significant: the US had a lot more knowledge than the USSR.

Following the successful trip made by John Glenn in February 1962, Khrushchev finally reached out to discuss a more collaborative effort. The two sides began to talk, leading to an agreement that they would work together in three keep areas:

1. The two sides would exchange weather data and have a coordinated launch effort for any meteorological satellites.

2. They would work together to map Earth's geomagnetic field.

3. They would make an effort toward experimental communications.

This work would benefit both nations since they were the only two countries capable of exploring space to any significant extent. Coordinated efforts to track the weather would provide them with safer launches and retrievals, and being able to communicate would potentially help avoid problems. The effort was not treated equally. The USSR classified everything as secret and rarely disclosed information to the US; the US tended to share their information. Even if it had not shared data with the USSR, the US tended to share data and knowledge with other nations, making the information easier for spies to find.

Following Khrushchev being pushed out of office in 1964, the next premier, Leonid Brezhnev, took a much stronger stance against the collaboration. Aware that the US was in a better position in terms of missile capabilities, he strove to create a force that would better rival what the Americans had achieved.

The next four years would see the USSR continue to fall behind the US, and they watched as Americans walked on the moon while they were far from capable of any similar achievement. Seeing that their dominance and superiority was over, the Soviets had more reasons to work with the US, though they had less leverage now that it was clear the US had progressed beyond their capabilities. Still, they were not willing to admit the current state of their program and changed their focus to establishing a robotic presence in space, which was much cheaper than sending people into space. The two space programs finally began to diverge as the US focused on developing better methods of traveling into space while the Soviets looked for better ways of remaining in space. Ultimately, this led to the US developing space shuttles while the USSR would eventually create a space station.

A movie called *Marooned* would ultimately help bring the two nations together. The plot of the movie had two Americans trapped in Earth's orbit being saved by Soviet cosmonauts. This fictitious image of how important a collaborative effort between the two was essential for success resonated within the small space community, and scientists on both sides saw the value of working together. After all, not many people on the planet had the knowledge necessary to help, and with few people in space, helping each other made more sense than perishing out of pride. A new push for working together came in 1975 via the Apollo-Soyuz Test Project, a docking mission that would successfully occur in July. After the successful docking, a bilateral working group was established to further develop a more collaborative effort between the two nations. However, this would not last long. President Jimmy Carter ended the cooperation, believing the USSR had obtained technology during the 1975 project. The two sides had begun to work more closely in other scientific fields, particularly life sciences and biomedical, but it would be several more years before they would make a more serious effort to combine their efforts in space.

The US had begun a program to examine other planets, largely staying out of space between 1975 and 1981. During this time, it was developing a space shuttle that would give astronauts better control over their flight during the landing process. The Soviets may not have traveled as much during this time, but they had sent cosmonauts to spend extended periods of time in space and learn about its effects on the body. This was knowledge the US did not have, as their longest missions up to that point were brief. As each nation had its own specialties, there was more communication between the two during the 1980s. Their relationship was still tense, but the Space Race tension had largely cooled. Having developed a friendlier relationship, the US and USSR worked together to study Halley's comet, a celestial object that comes close enough to be seen with the naked eye once every seventy-five years. Since the Soviets had more experience in space in recent years, they would use their own craft to study it from space while the US provided support from Earth. The US collected data about the comet as it drew close while the USSR and other nations in the Interagency Consultative Group participated in their mission (Vega 1 and 2 and the Giotto mission, respectively). The coordinated effort was very successful.

In 1984, President Ronald Reagan announced that NASA would begin developing a space station that would rival what the Soviet Union had accomplished, and he asked other nations to join. The USSR was excluded from this invitation, but there were talks with them behind the scenes. The US would more openly call for collaboration in October of that year. With the emergence of Mikhail Gorbachev as the new leader of the USSR, it appeared that this might finally be achieved in a more meaningful, long-term way.

Initially, the Soviets remained resistant to the idea that space and the military should be separated (the space program was always a part of the USSR military efforts). Following the explosion of the US space shuttle *Challenger* in January 1986, the USSR would find success when they launched part of what would later become the Mir space station less than a month later. With this achievement, they finally agreed to split their space efforts from their military work, though it is not known exactly what drove this decision. The two nations then established a five-year agreement by which they would coordinate several different projects (though none related to humans in space). In 1988, Regan was invited to join Gorbachev at the Kremlin. During Reagan's stay in the Soviet Union, Gorbachev tried to get him to agree to a joint effort to finally put a person on Mars. More than three decades later, this effort has yet to come to pass.

Conclusion

Though it wasn't intentionally started, the Space Race quickly became a heavy focus of both the US and USSR, the two superpowers that emerged after World War II. As nations began the long recovery process from the most destructive war in human history, the Allies quickly learned just how much more advanced the Nazis had been in terms of their weaponry and technology. The mistrust between most Allied nations and the USSR caused the rapid deterioration of cooperation, then more contentious and hostile interactions between the US and USSR became. This led to them each absorbing German scientists, most of whom had been a part of the Nazi Party, into their scientific communities. These Germans had been a part of many projects, including the development of an early ballistic missile. Though the USSR had a highly talented and knowledgeable scientist who was working space travel, the addition of the German scientists helped to speed up his work. The US would greatly benefit from their German scientists, as well.

As tensions between the US and USSR grew, they began to look for ways to show their superiority. Since the US had managed to be the first to develop nuclear weapons, it felt confident it was more advanced than its communist adversary. This led to complacency toward its current technology, especially as the cost of simply getting a satellite into space ballooned. This lasted until the surprising successful launch of *Sputnik 1*. As it passed over the US several times a day, it became clear that the US was already far behind the USSR, which had launched Sputnik in 1957. After that success, both nations increased their efforts to achieve a host of firsts, including getting the first person into space and back.

After several years of accomplishing a steady string of successes, the USSR would begin to falter in the Space Race, particularly after the death of Sergei Korolev in early 1966. Though the Soviet Union would achieve another major milestone by landing *Luna 9* on the moon, it was based on Korolev's work and was its last major success.

For nearly a decade, the Soviet Union had been the leader in most aspects of the Space Race. On July 16, 1969, the US launched *Apollo 11*, resulting in the successful landing of two men on the moon, followed by the crew's safe return. The US would make several more trips to the moon, but the USSR would never match this goal. While it was not the end of the Space Race, the USSR continued to fall behind the US in terms of achievements. Their space program officially ended in 1991.

Other countries had participated in the Space Race, largely working with NASA. Over time, the US and USSR also worked together. This led to much faster progress with things such as the Hubble Telescope and the International Space Station. Unfortunately, without that push, the drive to advance space travel and exploration largely died down during the 1990s. There were some staggering advancements, such as the exploration of Mars by the Mars Exploration Rover, but the pace at which those achievements were reached was much slower than expected. Considering that the US and USSR had first launched a satellite into space in 1957, then managed to land people on the moon by the end of the next decade, there were high expectations that people would be traveling to Mars by the end of the century. Without a serious driver, though, many nations began to decide to put their money toward other efforts. Only during the early 21st century would there be another push to see how far space exploration could be advanced. Nations that had little to do with the first Space Race have begun to more aggressively pursue a presence in space, most notably China, India, and Japan. Some have called this the New Space Race. There has also been a push by private companies to explore space. Since the slow of the original Space Race, these companies seem interested in ensuring that the pace of space exploration continues at a more rapid rate than it has since the 1970s.

Here's another book by Captivating History that you might like

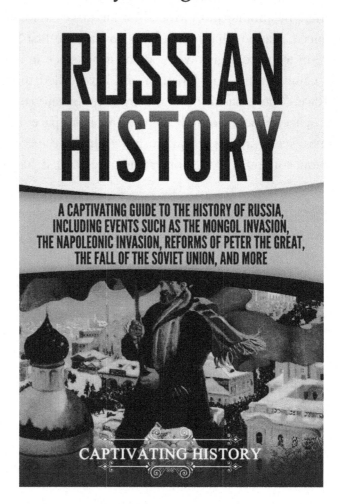

Free Bonus from Captivating History (Available for a Limited time)

Hi History Lovers!

Now you have a chance to join our exclusive history list so you can get your first history ebook for free as well as discounts and a potential to get more history books for free! Simply visit the link below to join.

Captivatinghistory.com/ebook

Also, make sure to follow us on Facebook, Twitter and Youtube by searching for Captivating History.

Bibliography

1957–58: The Year of the Satellite, NOAA, 2020, Satellite and Information Service, www.nesdis.noaa.gov/

60 years ago, Soviets launch Sputnik 3, Melanie Whiting, May 15, 2018, NASA, www.nasa.gov/

60 Years Ago: Vanguard Fails to Reach Orbit, Mark Garcia, December 6, 2017, NASA, www.nasa.gov/

A look at people killed during space missions, Seth Borenstien, November 1, 2014, Science X Network, phys.org/

A Visual History of Spacewalks, Jeffery Kluger, June 3, 2015, Time Magazine, time.com/

Alouette I and II, Canadian Space Agency, September 28, 2018, www.asc-csa.gc.ca/

An Early History of Satellites Timeline, Broadband Wherever, 2020, NASA, www.jpl.nasa.gov/

Apollo 11: First Men on the Moon, Nola Taylor Redd, May 9, 2019, Future US Inc, www.space.com/

Car crashes, curses, and carousing—the story of the second Soviet in space, Emily Carney, June 16, 2016, arstechnica, arstechnica.com/

Challenger: The Shuttle Disaster That Changed NASA, Elizabeth Howell, May 1, 2019, Future US Inc, www.space.com/

Cosmic Menagerie: A History of Animals in Space, Karl Tate, April 17, 2013, Future US Inc, www.space.com/

Deaths associated with US space programs, January 4, 2019, Airsafe.com, www.airsafe.com/

Development History, Anatoly Zak, 2020, www.russianspaceweb.com/

Did Politics Fuel the Space Race?, Robert Longely, March 20, 2020, Thought Co., www.thoughtco.com/

Explorer 1 Overview, Sarah Loff, Brian Dunbar, August 3, 2017, NASA, www.nasa.gov/

Explorer 1: The First U.S. Satellite, Elizaabeth Howell, August 11, 2017, www.space.com/

'Flight, We Are Docked!' Gemini 8 Achieved 1st Space Docking 50 Years Ago, Robert Z. Pearlman, March 16, 2016, Future US Inc, www.space.com/

From Monkey To Man, Gale, 2020, Cenagage Company, www.gale.com/

Gherman Stepanovich Titov, The Editors of Encyclopaedia Britannica, 2020, Britannica, www.britannica.com/

How NASA Works, Craig Freudenrich, Patrick J. Kiger, 2020, howstuffworks, science.howstuffworks.com/

International Geophysical Year, The Editors of Encyclopedia Britannica, 2020, Encyclopedia Britannica, www.britannica.com/

JFK's 'Moon Speech' Still Resonates 50 Years Later, Mike Wall, September 12, 2012, Future US Inc, www.space.com/

Laika the Dog & the First Animals in Space, Elizabeth Dohrer, May 31, 2017, Future US Inc, www.space.com/

Luna 01, NASA, February 13, 2018, solarsystem.nasa.gov/

Luna 1, Dr. David R. Williams, May 14, 2020, NASA, nssdc.gsfc.nasa.gov/

Lunar Lost & Found: The Search for Old Spacecraft, Leonard David, March 27, 2006, Future US Inc, www.space.com/

March 16, 1966: Gemini's First Docking of Two Spacecraft in Earth Orbit, Sarah Loff, August 6, 2017, NASA, www.nasa.gov/

Missions, Mars Exploration Program, 2020, NASA, mars.nasa.gov/

Moon landing anniversary: How did the historic space race play out?, Lauren Chadwick, July 20, 2019, EuronNews, www.euronews.com/

NASA's Origins & the Dawn of the Space Age, NASA, 2020, history.nasa.gov/

Only Three People Have Died in Space, Amy Shira Teitel, August 20, 2017, Discover, www.discovermagazine.com/

Origins of the Cold War in Europe, Robert Wilde, September 8, 2017, ThoughtCo, www.thoughtco.com/

Profile of John Glenn, Brain Dunbar, August 3, 2017, NASA, www.nasa.gov/

Remembering Belka and Strelka, Tony Reichhardt, August 19, 2010, Air & Space Magazine, www.airspacemag.com/

Roscosmos: Russia's Space Agency, Elizabeth Howell, January 20, 2018, Future US Inc, www.space.com/

Sept. 9, 1955: DoD Picks Vanguard To Launch U.S. Satellite, SpaceNews Editor, June 29, 2004, SpaceNews, spacenews.com/

Sergei Korolev: Father of the Soviet Union's Success in Space, August 3, 2007, European Space Agency, www.esa.int/

Space Race Timeline, Royal Museums Greenwich, 2020, www.rmg.co.uk/

Space Race, Space Next, 2020, Encyclopedia Britannica, www.britannica.com/

Space Race: The Space Rivalry between the United States and Soviet Union and Its Aftermath, Smithsonian, 2020, airandspace.si.edu/

Sputnik 1, Dr. David R. Williams, September 3, 2020, NASA, nssdc.gsfc.nasa.gov/

Sputnik 1, NASA Content Administrator, August 7, 2017, NASA, www.nasa.gov/

Sputnik, 1957, Foreign Service Institute, 2020, Office of the Historian, history.state.gov/

Sputnik: How the World's 1st Artificial Satellite Worked (Infographic), Karl Tate, October 4, 2012, Future US Inc, www.space.com/

Sputnik: The Space Race's Opening Shot, Elizabeth Howell, August 22, 2018, Space.com, www.space.com/

The Apollo Program (1963 - 1972), Dr. David R. Williams, September 16, 2013, NASA, nssdc.gsfc.nasa.gov/

The Gemini Program (1962 - 1966), Dr. David R. Williams, December 30, 2004, NASA, nssdc.gsfc.nasa.gov/

The Launch of Sputnik, 1957, U.S. Department of State, January 20, 2009, 2001-2009.state.gov/

The Luna 1 Hoax Hoax, Tony Reichhardt, January 2, 2013, Air & Space Magazine, www.airspacemag.com/

The Moon and Man at 50: Why JFK's Space Exploration Speech Still Resonates, Mike Wall, May 25, 2011, Future US Inc, www.space.com/

The Sad, Sad Story of Laika, the Space Dog, and Her One-Way Trip into Orbit, Alice George, April 11, 2018, Smithsonian Magazine, www.smithsonianmag.com/

The Soviet Manned Lunar Program, Marcus Lindroos, 2020, FAS, fas.org/

The Soviet Union is first to the Moon, Richard Cavendish, September 9, 2009, History Today, www.historytoday.com/

The Space Race And Man On The Moon, Times Reporter, August 28, 2010, The New Times, www.newtimes.co.rw/

The Space Race of the 1960s, Martin Kelly, March 26, 2020, Thought Co., www.thoughtco.com/

The Space Race, American Experience, 2020, www.pbs.org/

The Space Race, Michael Kernan, August 1997, Smithsonian Magazine, www.smithsonianmag.com/

The Space Race: How Cold War Tensions Put a Rocket under the Quest for the Moon, Science Focus Magazine, 2020, Immediate Media, www.sciencefocus.com/

The Start of the Space Race, Khan Academy, 2020, www.khanacademy.org/

This Is Why Sputnik Crashed Back To Earth After Only 3 Months, Ethan Siegel, November 15, 2018, Starts with a Bang, Forbes

This Is Why The Soviet Union Lost 'The Space Race' To The USA, Ethan Siegel, July 11, 2019, Forbes, www.forbes.com/

This Month in Physics History, American Physical Society, 2020, www.aps.org/

Today in science: 1st spacecraft to moon, Earthsky, January 2, 2017, earthsky.org/

United States-Soviet Space Cooperation during the Cold War, Roald Sagdeev, Susan Eisenhower, 2020, NASA, www.nasa.gov/

Vega 1 & 2, Ron Baalke, 2020, Comets, stardust.jpl.nasa.gov/

Wernher von Braun and the Nazis, Michael J. Neufeld, 2020, American Experience, PBS, www.pbs.org/

Wernher von Braun: History's Most Controversial Figure?, Amy Shira Teitel, May 3, 2013, Aljazeera, www.aljazeera.com/

What Was the Space Race?, Adam Mann, August 7, 2019, FutureUS Inc, www.space.com/

Who Was John Glenn?, Brain Dunbar, August 6, 2017, NASA, www.nasa.gov/

Why the U.S. Government Brought Nazi Scientists to America after World War II, Danny Lewis, November 16, 2016, Smithsonian Magazine, www.smithsonianmag.com

Why Yuri Gagarin Remains the First Man in Space, Even Though He Did Not Land Inside His Spacecraft, Cathleen Lewis, April 20, 2010, Smithsonian, airandspace.si.edu/

Will Hitler Be the First Person That Aliens See?, Ross Pomery, September 19, 2013, Real Clear Science, www.realclearscience.com/

Women of NASA, National Geographic, March 2, 2020, National Geographic Society, www.nationalgeographic.org/

Yuri Gagarin: First Man in Space, Jim Wilson, April 13, 2011, NASA, www.nasa.gov/

Yuri Gagarin: First Man in Space, Nola Taylor Redd,
October 12, 2018, Future US Inc, www.space.com/

Now that this book has come to its conclusion, let's take a moment
to reflect on some of the reading and reference materials that
helped make this text possible. Here you will find a wide variety of
topics as it pertains to the geopolitical conflict that came to be
known as the Cold War.

The United States in the Cold War: 1945-1989. Christopher
Collier.

Reagan and Gorbachev: How the Cold War Ended. Jack F.
Matlock, Jr.

*When the World Seemed New: George H. W. Bush and the End
of the Cold War.* Jeffrey A. Engel.

*The Cold War and After: History, Theory, and the Logic of
International Politics.* Marc Trachtenberg.

*Dealing with Dictators: The United States, Hungary, and East
Central Europe, 1942-1989.* Laszlo Borhi.

*Empowering Revolution: America, Poland, and the End of the
Cold War.* Gregory F. Domber.

*A Covert Action: Reagan, The CIA, And the Cold War Struggle in
Poland.* Seth G. Jones.

A History of Modern Ethiopia: 1855-1991. Bahru Zewde.

Made in the USA
Coppell, TX
09 December 2020

43897338R00125